FERRARI
The Legend

FERRARI
The Legend

Mark Konig

p

Page 1: Ferrari F40 petrol filler cap; one is located on each side, and this British-made component incorporates a pressure blow-off device. Page 2: Dino 246 GTS. This example was supplied by Maranello Concessionaires and is fitted with non-standard accessory perspex headlamp covers and a chromed steel nudge bar. Page 3: 365 GTC4 is unusual in red, but still a much underrated car.

This is a Parragon book
This edition published in 2004

Copyright © Parragon 1997

Parragon
Queen Street House
4 Queen Street
Bath BA1 1HE, UK

Designed, produced and packaged by
Stonecastle Graphics Ltd

Edited by Philip de Ste. Croix

ISBN: 1-40542-692-6

Printed in Indonesia

Photographic credits:

All photographs by **Neill Bruce Motoring Photolibrary**, with the exception of the following:
(Abbreviations: r = right, l = left, t = top, b = below)

Peter Roberts Collection/Neill Bruce: 7(*t*), 7(*b*), 77(*b*).

Keith Bluemel: 15(*t*), 15(*b*), 22, 24(*b*), 24-25(*b*), 28, 29, 41(*b*), 43(*t*), 45(*t*).

Figures and data in this book are generally quoted in metric measurements first, with the Imperial equivalents noted in brackets.

Neill Bruce and the publishers would like to thank the many owners who have made their cars available for photography, including the following:

Brooks Auctioneers: Blue 250 Tour de France; 410 Superamerica; 250 GTE 2+2; 250 GT Lusso and 330 GT 2+2.

Duncan Hamilton Ltd: 275 GTB 'longnose', 250 GT California and 365 GTC4.

Moto Technique Ltd: 365 GT 2+2.

The Earl of March for the wonderful Goodwood Festival of Speed.

Also special thanks to Alan Mapp of Maranello Concessionaires Ltd., who spent many days placing cars in the right position in the 1970s and '80s. To Great Fosters restaurant in Egham for allowing photography in their grounds for over 20 years, and to Adrian Hall, for lending me his beautiful grounds, and letting me photograph his Dino and Daytona.

Contents

Introduction

ENZO FERRARI, when he died in 1988, was one of the best known men in the world, a superstar. His fame, which was greater than politicians, movie stars or pop idols earning him the sobriquet 'Pope of the north', was created by his cars, after which everyone yearns but few can afford. To some he was know as 'that great agitator of men' for pushing engineers to design faster cars and for tempting drivers to go to the edge. It isn't necessarily a question of taste that precludes the female form from adorning Ferrari's cars at Motor Shows; they really don't need it, it is as simple as that. Crowds form to gawk at one parked by the kerb, crowds surge against barriers at Motor Shows, the tifosi (the fans) throng the stands at motor races cheering their heroes on. To the tifosi Ferrari is a religion.

Enzo Anselmo Ferrari, Dott. Ing., was born in 1898 in Modena, the son of a metal worker. One of his first jobs before the First World War intervened was as sports writer for *La Gazzetta dello Sport*.

During the war he served in the 3rd Mountain Artillery as a farrier. Ill health predominated during this period of his life. After the war his obsession with cars began and whilst working in Milan with CMN (Construzione Mecchanicale Nazionale) he competed in his first motor races. Soon Enzo Ferrari was to join Alfa Romeo as a test driver and achieve a memorable 2nd place in the 1920 Targa Florio. Alfa Romeo team cars were run under the Scuderia Ferrari banner from 1930 to 1938 with great success. The 815, a sports car built by Auto Avio Construzione, Ferrari's own engineering company which was run from the Scuderia Ferrari headquarters in Modena, made one appearance before the Second World War brought racing to a standstill. War and racing have some common ground; brave drivers take huge risks and technical progress is spurred on by the need for survival. Ferrari moved to the village of Maranello a few miles out of Modena during the war but failed to avoid Allied bombs. In 1946 Ferrari hired Gioachino Colombo and together they realized Enzo's dream when the first V12 Ferrari racing car drove onto the track in 1947. The first road car, the 166, arrived in 1948 and it had a 2 litre V12 engine. Ever since then Ferrari road cars have been much sought after for their stunning performance, glamorous appearance and racing pedigree.

Left: Enzo Ferrari, on the extreme left, pictured at the Fiorano Circuit at Maranello in 1973 during a factory visit by United Kingdom Ferrari importers Colonel Ronnie Hoare (foreground) and Shaun Bealey (right), together with long-serving press officer Dott. Franco Gozzi.

Right: Motoring history in the making at Monza in August 1923 – left to right, Giorgio Rimini, Nicola Romeo and Enzo Ferrari.

Below: Sicily, 1920, before the start of the Targa Florio, Enzo Ferrari sits at the wheel of his Alfa Romeo (centre) in which he was to finish second.

Ferrari 166 & 195 Inter

THE FIRST cars sold by Ferrari for use on the road were directly evolved from racing cars. The 166 with a 2 litre V12 engine was itself derived from the 125 which was the first V12 to be made by Enzo Ferrari's new factory in Maranello. The Ferrari 166 V12 was built with a 60 degree V and a single overhead camshaft per bank operating inclined valves via roller rockers; the cam shafts were driven by chain from the seven main bearing crankshaft and all the main castings were in aluminium. The first 166 Inter was seen at the Turin Motor Show in 1948; it was a two-door coupé bodied by Touring.

In May 1948 the Ferrari 166 berlinetta (a little saloon car) with coachwork by Allemano gave Clemente Biondetti his fourth, and Ferrari's first, Mille Miglia victory. The great road races of Europe were where Enzo Ferrari had been brought up, and one of his successes was second place in the Targa Florio of 1920. The Targa Florio was a dream race, 72 kilometres (45 miles) of country road on the north coast of Sicily with twisting mountain hairpins and narrow straights following the coast. It is hardly surprising that the main effort of Ferrari's new factory was directed towards winning these classic road races. From 1948 until 1957, when the Mille Miglia came to an abrupt halt, Ferrari won it eight times. One of the more remarkable Ferrari results came in the 1950 Mille Miglia when Giannino Marzotto, aged 22, brought the 195S home to victory wearing an immaculate blue suit. The Marzotto family owned a textile business among various other interests and no fewer than four brothers drove Ferraris in the Mille Miglia of 1950.

The 166 seen at Turin in 1948 had a chassis made by GILCO, which had been developed by Gilberto Colombo (no relation of the Ferrari engine designer) and Ferrari from oval-section steel tubing in the form of two side members upswept at the back over the rear axle with internal cross braces.

Below: Ferrari 166 Inter with rather heavy coachwork by Carrozzeria Touring. Few Ferraris had these steel wheels.

To this was attached independent suspension at the front by upper and lower arms and a transverse leaf spring. The Houdaille hydraulic shock absorbers formed the inner attachment points for the upper arms of the front suspension. The right-hand-drive steering was by worm and wheel and two short track rods and, at the rear, a rigid axle was suspended on semi elliptical springs. A 5-speed gearbox was contained in an all-alloy ribbed casting and driven by a single plate clutch. Borani disc wheels with alloy rims and hub caps with Ferrari letters stamped on them completed the chassis.

Ferrari does not make car bodies at Maranello and never has. The Scaglietti works in Modena, now wholly owned by Ferrari, and Pininfarina in Turin do all the current coachwork. (Pinin Farina is the man who gave his name to the company which subsequently changed its name to Pininfarina in the late 1950s). The 166 and 195 bodies were built by the leading specialists which included Touring, Vignale, Ghia, Bertone and Allemano, all of whom were (or still are) based in the industrial north of Italy.

In late 1950 the 195 Inter was introduced – this was the road version of the 2.3 litre V12 so ably demonstrated by Marzotto and others in races. The 195 used a double choke Weber 36 DCF carburettor with a compression ratio of 7.5:1 and produced 25bhp more than the 166.

Production figures	In production	Total produced
166 Inter	1948-50	36
195 Inter	1950-52	27

SPECIFICATION	166 INTER	195 INTER
ENGINE	60° V12, 1995cc	60° V12, 2340cc
HORSEPOWER	105bhp @ 6000rpm	130bhp @ 6000rpm
TRANSMISSION	Manual 5-speed	Manual 5-speed
CHASSIS	Steel tubular	Steel tubular
SUSPENSION	Independent front, rigid rear axle *(both models)*	
BRAKES	Drum	Drum
TOP SPEED	193km/h (120mph)	201km/h (125mph)
ACCELERATION	0-96km/h (60mph): 10sec 0-161km/h (100mph): 25sec	N/A N/A

Above: The businesslike cockpit of the Ferrari 166 Inter.

Below: 195 Inter with more sporting Touring coachwork.

9

Ferrari 212 Inter

FOR THIS model, Colombo's V12 engine was bored again giving a capacity of 212cc per cylinder and thus 2.6 litres. Fewer than 100 Ferrari 212 Inters were made from its introduction at the Brussels Motor Show in l951 until production ceased in 1953. Ferrari at this time was still predominantly a racing car manufacturer and the road cars were made very much to order. The 212 chassis was bodied by several of the top Italian coachbuilders and there were few runs of identical cars.

The Vignale designs were very sporting and more often than not actually used in competition, although the 212 Export was the version intended for racing. These early cars were nearly always right-hand-drive as racing circuits are usually right handed and the driver prefers to sit on the inside of a corner. The 212 Inter was bodied as coupé, cabriolet and spider. Pinin Farina made nearly twenty traditional-looking 212 coupés and this contract formed the early foundations of the

relationship between the two firms. The first Pinin Farina-bodied Ferrari was a 212 cabriolet, chassis no 0177E. This was a rather heavy looking, seriously grand, two-seater – it had a chromed 'egg crate' grille, full width chrome bumpers and two air intakes on the bonnet.

Ferrari 212 Inters also had coachwork by Ghia, who built a handsome 2+2 for the Turin Salon of 1952. Carrozzeria Touring had produced exciting closed bodywork for the 166 and 195 Ferraris for road and track, but by the time the 212 came out their association with Ferrari had begun to fade. The best known 212 by Touring must be a coupé with a glass panel in the roof named 'Aerlux'. Even in 1952 this car still had a two-piece front screen. The interior of a Ferrari 212, whoever built it, had a characteristic dashboard with two large analogue gauges: the left one gave speed, mileometer, oil pressure and fuel gauge information. The right-hand one was a combination of revolution counter, time clock and water temperature gauge. The driving position was dominated by the alloy spoke steering wheel – the wooden rim often inlaid with a contrasting coloured wood. Engine turned spokes radiated from the famous yellow horn button with a black prancing horse emblem mounted on it.

The chassis of the first 212 had a strange rear suspension incorporating two semi-elliptical leaf springs on each side and three universal joints in the drive line – soon to give way to the excellent system of a single leaf spring with radius arms top and

Left: Ferrari 212 Export, chassis # 0111S, with body by Vignale pictured in the grounds of Brocket Hall.

SPECIFICATION	212 INTER
ENGINE	60° V12, 2562cc
HORSEPOWER	150/170bhp @ 6500rpm
TRANSMISSION	Manual 5 speed
CHASSIS	Steel tubular
SUSPENSION	Independent front, rigid rear axle
BRAKES	Drum
TOP SPEED	199km/h (123.5mph)
ACCELERATION	0-96km/h (60mph): 7.05sec 0-161km/h (100mph): 18.1sec

Panamericana. The cars were driven by Luigi Chinetti/Piero Taruffi and Alberto Ascari/Luigi Villoresi. These were SEFAC works cars run by Centro Deportivo Italiano and their 1-2 victory was a potent advertising coup for the rich North American market. The importer, none other than Luigi Chinetti himself, went from strength to strength.

Production figures	In production	Total produced
212 Inter	1951-53	80

Right: Interior of a 212 Export by Vignale features polished wood and aluminium together with hand-stitched leather.
Below: 212 Export showing Vignale's unique rear lights.

bottom on each side. The chassis was built by Gilberto Colombo in Milan from oval-section steel tube of a generous size. Independent front suspension used a transverse leaf spring with radius arms top and bottom on each side. Houdaille lever arm shock absorbers were to be found at each corner and the unassisted steering was by worm and gear.

All 212 Inters had the same basic twelve cylinder engine designed by Gioachino Colombo, initially fitted with a single twin-choke Weber carburettor. It gave 150bhp at 6500rpm. This engine appeared to be quite long and low but the height from inlet manifold to the top of the carburettor air cleaner necessitated quite a high bonnet line. Later versions of the 212 Inter had three double-choke Webers and gave 170bhp at 6500rpm. Both versions had 5-speed gearboxes, and it is interesting to note that in the factory brochure of 1952 the fuel consumption is quoted as nearly 19 miles to the gallon (6.6km/l).

The most important achievement of the 212 was undoubtedly its 1-2 victory in the 1951 Carrera

Ferrari 340, 342 America, 375 & 250 Europa

AURELIO Lampredi designed Ferrari's second V12 engine for the Grand Prix cars of 1950-51. This was the 'long block' V12, eventually of 4493cc, giving up to 380bhp at 7500rpm. During the evolution of this engine a 4101cc version was made, and the sports car engine was a direct development of this. Most of the 340s were sports racing cars, but eight were designed and built for the road.

As was usual in the '50s, several coachbuilders made bodies, including Touring Vignale and Ghia. The Lampredi engine is recognized externally from Colombo's V12 in several ways, such as the seven studs holding down the cam cover's lower edge compared with Colombo's six, together with some external water and oil pipes at the front of the block. The roadgoing 340s had civilized coachwork, but the chassis and engine were similar to the

competition cars and there was no synchromesh on the 5-speed gearbox. The 340 America, as the new car was called, won the 1951 Mille Miglia wearing a coupé body by Vignale and driven by Luigi Villoresi. This was a wonderful transition period at Ferrari when road and race cars really did get mixed up and were made alongside each other on the same assembly line. As a general rule, Ferrari racing cars have been assigned even numbers for their chassis numbers and the road cars the odd ones (or so it was until 1988). Like most things at Ferrari, however, there are exceptions, and the 340 and 342 all had even numbers. A beautiful example of a 340 roadcar was a cabriolet built by Vignale on chassis number 0138A which tragically was dismembered by its owner, Lord Brocket, in the early 1990s as part of an insurance fraud.

At the Brussels Motor Show in January 1951, the new 342 was announced. This was a more refined road version of the 340; it retained the same sized engine but lost 20bhp, the wheelbase was lengthened and the gearbox lost a ratio and gained synchromesh. Only six 342s were built. By now Pinin Farina was Ferrari's preferred coachbuilder, making three coupés and two cabriolets; the sixth car was a Vignale cabriolet.

The Paris show of 1953 saw the debut of the 375, which replaced the 342, and also the new 250

Left: 340 America, chassis # 0082, the winner of the 1951 Mille Miglia, at the 1994 Goodwood Festival of Speed.

SPECIFICATION	340 A	342 A	375 A	250 Europa
ENGINE	V12, 4101cc	V12, 4101cc	V12, 4523cc	V12, 2963cc
HORSEPOWER	220bhp @ 6000rpm	200bhp @ 5000rpm	300bhp @ 6300rpm	200bhp @ 6000rpm
TRANSMISSION	Manual 5-speed	Manual 4-speed	Manual 4-speed	Manual 4-speed
CHASSIS	Steel tubular	Steel tubular	Steel tubular	Steel tubular
SUSPENSION	Independent front, rigid rear axle *(all models)*			
BRAKES	Drum	Drum	Drum	Drum
TOP SPEED	241km/h (150mph)	241km/h (150mph)	249km/h (155mph)	217km/h (135mph)
ACCELERATION	N/A	N/A	N/A	N/A

Europa which used the smallest version of the Lampredi engine. Both cars had a very similar chassis of 2800mm (9ft 2in) wheelbase, needlessly long for the three litre but done in the interests of rationalization. The 375 was a very grand car and sold only to the 'rich and famous'. Pinin Farina bodied the majority with coupé bodies, though the 375 cabriolet built by Ferrari for King Leopold of the Belgians would surely feature prominently in any list of the most wanted cars ever built. Owners of 375s included Emperor Bo Dia of Thailand, Giovanni Agnelli (boss of Fiat), and film supremo Roberto Rosellini.

The 250 Europa, by contrast, quickly faded. The chassis was too heavy for three litres and the engine was physically too big for only three litres swept volume. Future engines of this size would be developments of Colombo's original V12.

Right: Interior of 340 America, chassis # 0082, showing elegant three spoke, wood-rimmed wheel and amber-coloured gear lever knob. Below: Another shot at Goodwood, showing the classic lines of Vignale's coupé body.

Production figures	In production	Total produced
340 A	1951-52	8
342 A	1952-53	6
375 A	1953-54	12
250 Europa	1953-54	about 20

Ferrari 250 MM, 250 Europa GT & 250 GT

AFTER THE 212 and the 250 Europa, the stage was set for Colombo's V12, 2953cc engine. This started the way it meant to continue. Giovanni Bracco won the 1952 Mille Miglia driving a 250 prototype on its first outing. Most further examples of this car were also racing cars but at least two were built for the road. They were know as 250 MM. The MM had a steel tubular chassis with independent front suspension using a transverse leaf spring and Houdaille lever-arm shock absorbers. The rear axle was located with two radius arms on each side and sprung by semi-elliptical springs. Three 36 IF 4C Weber carburettors helped produce 240bhp at 7200rpm. The 250 Europe GT was first seen at the Paris Salon in 1954. The coachwork of this example

by Pinin Farina was a development of the 250 Europa. This, however, was a new car with a new chassis and the 3 litre Colombo V12 engine. The shorter wheelbase – 2600mm (8ft 6in) – and revised rear suspension made for a better handling and more manoeuvrable car, though still fitted with a transverse leaf spring in the front suspension. Vignale bodied at least one 250 Europa GT with a coupé body using a Chevrolet Corvette windscreen. This car was built for Princess Liliana de Rethy of Belgium – a long-time Ferrari enthusiast. The Colombo-designed 3 litre engine developed 220bhp at 7000rpm which was enough to propel the Europa GT up to 225km/h (140mph). The shorter wheelbase, reduced weight and the more refined

coachwork of the (Europa) GT was the foundation of the range of cars which were to make Ferrari famous, not just in the eyes of those who could afford them but with a much wider worldwide audience too.

Pinin Farina continued to hone the 250 shape and at the Geneva Motor Show in 1956 the new 250 GT was shown. The body of this car was sub-contracted to be built by Boano who also built a cabriolet on the same chassis. Generally, when a Ferrari designed by Pinin Farina was sub-contracted to another coachbuilder, the designer's badge was used to identify the coachbuilder, though some Boano-badged examples were made. This was also true of later examples when Boano and his son-in-law Ezio Ellena merged to become Boano/Ellena. Mechanical improvements continued all the time.

Many people today would be surprised at the low level of luxury to be found in the 250 series cars. Such items as painted dashboards, thin carpets and unlined boots all appealed to the sporting customers whose main concern was that it would pull maximum revs in top gear. The chassis, still made from oval-section steel tubes, now had independent coil-spring front suspension and the rear axle was located with two pairs of radius arms. In the original sales brochure there was a choice of five rear-axle ratios, the highest one claiming a top speed of 253km/h (157mph) at 7000rpm. This

Left: Ferrari 250 MM, chassis # 0340.

SPECIFICATION	250 MM	250 Europa GT	250 GT
ENGINE	V12, 2953cc	V12, 2953cc	V12, 2953cc
HORSEPOWER	240bhp @ 7200rpm	220bhp @ 7000rpm	240bhp @ 7000rpm
TRANSMISSION	Manual 4-speed	Manual 4-speed	Manual 4-speed
CHASSIS	Steel tubular	Steel tubular	Steel tubular
SUSPENSION	Independent front, rigid rear axle *(all models)*		
BRAKES	Drum	Drum	Drum
TOP SPEED	254km/h (158mph)	225km/h (140mph)	209km/h (130mph)
ACCELERATION	0-96km/h (60mph): N/A 0-161km/h (100mph): N/A	5.9sec 15.5sec	6sec 15sec

Production figures	In production	Total produced
250 MM	1953-54	2 road cars
250 Europa GT	1954-55	35
250 GT	1956-58	about 130

seems unlikely even with 240bhp on tap. The acceleration times given in the accompanying table were established with the lowest final drive ratio which gave a maximum speed at 7000rpm of 203km/h (126mph). Behind the leather covered seats was a luggage platform equipped with straps to secure cases. Borani wire wheels carried 6.00 x 16in tyres.

The Turin Show in 1958 saw the introduction of the definitive 250 GT 'Ellena' coupé. This coupé body had a higher roof line to improve access and visibility. There were no quarter light windows. The Boano and Ellena cars were undoubtedly the first 'production' Ferrari cars. They were mostly similar and 50 out of a total of about 130 were built by Ellena. As a production model it was not intended to be used in competition, but there were several notable successes including overall victory in the 1957 Acropolis Rally, and a class win in the 1956 Alpine Rally. On both occasions the car was driven by Jean Estager.

Mechanical improvements for 1957 included larger brakes and the adoption of a new steering

box made by the German company Z-F. Whilst the Boano and Ellena creations could be termed 'production', the same chassis was bodied by Pinin Farina with several styles of cabriolet, some of which were owned by well known people, including English Ferrari works driver Peter Collins, well-known 1950s racing driver Porfirio Rubirosa, Count Volpi and Prince Sadrudin Aga Khan.

Above: Ferrari 250 GT Boano, chassis # 0533 GT.
Below: Ferrari 250 GT Europa, chassis # 0399 GT.

Ferrari 250 GT Tour de France & California

THE GRAND Touring class in international long-distance racing began to be highly competitive in the mid '50s. The Mercedes Benz 300 SL gull-wing coupé, various Jaguar, Lancia, Alfa Romeo and Aston Martins, all competed with Ferrari for honours in the GT class. This class was so competitive and popular that the racing coupés were often placed in high positions overall in the races.

The racing berlinetta was an important car to Ferrari in two ways. Firstly, it was very successful and enhanced his name; and secondly, demand was such that he made good profits from their sales. To many people a street Ferrari looks a little spartan, without excess luxury, particularly when the price is considered. A racing berlinetta is really a sports racing car with a roof. It is totally devoid of trim, sound proofing, heating and other creature comforts. All glass with the exception of the front screen would be made of perspex and the body panels were nearly always aluminium. Luggage space was reduced to practically zero to accommodate enormous fuel tanks.

The early '55 berlinettas were evolutions of Pinin Farina prototypes and specials, though the first real Tour de France (as we now know them) was created by Scaglietti in Modena. This coachbuilder (a few minutes from Maranello) was often used for racing car bodies and modifications which needed carrying out in a hurry. The 250 Tour de France as built by Scaglietti was an all-aluminium berlinetta built on a regular steel tube chassis. The panels were supported by lightweight steel tubes. Most of the cars built had very successful competition careers. A few berlinettas received a modicum of trim and made sensational road cars. For winter driving a blind was pulled up by a small chrome chain to prevent cool air going through the water radiator. It could be lowered by the driver as the temperature rose. Some berlinettas had two foot-operated dip switches – one dipped the headlights in the normal way and the other was wired up to flash the lights and operate the powerful air horns at the same time. Beautiful hand-made wood-trimmed alloy steering wheels framed the famous prancing horse emblem in the centre of the wheel. Most berlinettas had non-adjustable bucket seats trimmed in leather. Hip hugging was necessary as seat belts hadn't arrived yet, nor had roll cages! The bonnet lid had no hinges in the interest of weight-saving and was held down with leather straps and inimitable chromed sprung catches (with which the unwary always scratch the paint).

Zagato, another Italian coachbuilder, made a number of 250 GT bodies. These are always recognized by the traditional 'double bubble' in the roof line. Scaglietti-bodied cars sometimes had

16

SPECIFICATION	250 TOUR DE FRANCE	250 GT LWB CALIFORNIA
ENGINE	V12, 2953cc	V12, 2953cc
HORSEPOWER	230/280bhp @ 7000rpm	240/250bhp @ 7000rpm
TRANSMISSION	Manual 4-speed	Manual 4-speed
CHASSIS	Steel tubular	Steel tubular
SUSPENSION	Independent front, rigid rear axle *(both models)*	
BRAKES	Drum	Drum
TOP SPEED	230km/h (143mph)	201km/h (125mph)
ACCELERATION	0-96km/h (60mph): 7.8sec	7.2sec
	0-161km/h (100mph): 16.1sec	16.4sec

headlights set back in the wings and covered by curved perspex covers. The panel behind the window glass on early cars was plain. In 1957 it acquired 14 small louvres, which were reduced to 3 large ones later in the year. In 1958 the definitive version had one large louvre. These features provide the easiest way of dating a Scaglietti berlinetta. From 1955-1959 the 250 GT berlinetta 'Tour de France' or 'long wheel base' was the most successful car in the GT category – Its mantle being taken over in 1960 with the introduction of the even more successful '250 GT short wheel base'. Pinin Farina designed an open version of the Tour de France in response to requests from Ferrari's North American importer Luigi Chinetti. This car was known as the 250 GT California and what a beautiful car it was. A number of these Scaglietti-built spiders were even raced with success, the best result being 8th overall at Sebring in 1960.

Opposite page: Ferrari 250 GT LWB, chassis # 0557 GT. Winner of the Tour de France in 1956.
Right and below: Ferrari 250 GT LWB California.

Production figures	In production	Total produced
250 Tour de France	1955-59	84
250 GT California	1957-60	49

*Above: 3-litre V12 engine of 250 GT T de F, chassis #
0677, which came 3rd in the 1957 Mille Miglia.*
Below: Racy three-quarter view of Scaglietti's berlinetta.

*Above: Cockpit of the same car looking like new, with no
unnecessary clutter, just asking to be driven.*
Right: The 250 GT LWB Tour de France, chassis # 0677.

18

Ferrari 410 Superamerica

SOMETIMES known as the 4.9, the 410 SA had the largest engine yet fitted to a roadgoing Ferrari. The Lampredi 60° V12 had a silumin crankcase with iron liners screwed into the cylinder head. This unit of cylinder head and block was bolted to the crankcase. There was no chance of a head gasket blowing because there wasn't one – but it required very precise engineering to achieve. Each cylinder head had an overhead camshaft operating two valves per cylinder via roller rockers. The cam covers (as usual for a Lampredi engine)

had seven nuts securing their lower edges as opposed to the six found on a contemporary Colombo V12. Three double-choke Weber 46 DCF/3 carburettors fed the 4.9 litres of thirsty Ferrari. Not that many owners knew or worried about it, but under 3.5km/lit (10mpg) was normal. The chassis was a typical Ferrari steel tube design incorporating oval-section tubes in the base. These oval-section tubes were made by Gilco Autotelai in Milan and have been almost a trademark of Ferrari chassis for many years.

The first 410 SA had wheelbase of 2800mm (9ft 2in), which was long but totally in keeping with the scale of this big car. The independent front suspension used forged steel wishbones, all attached to the chassis via bronze bushes and ground steel pins. Each joint had its own individual grease nipple which required frequent attention. Such attention was well worth it, as the lack of compliance in these suspension systems made for precise, positive and reassuring handling. The rear suspension was more or less conventional with semi-elliptical leaf springs and two radius arms on each side controlling a rigid axle, the aluminium nose piece of which accommodated the final drive ratio. This could be chosen from four available options prior to delivery.

The first time the 410 SA was seen in public was without coachwork on Ferrari's stand at the Paris Salon in 1955. It was next seen fully clothed by Pinin Farina at the Brussels Salon in 1956. The Pinin Farina design for this new car had its roots in the Boano-built 250 with a lowish sill line and large windows. A large grille behind the front wheel allowed hot air to escape from the engine compartment. Slim wrap-around bumpers, Borani wheels and a low air intake on the bonnet all added to a very distinguished looking car. As usual with cars built in such limited numbers, no two versions were identical in every detail, and one or two were very different, particularly the Ghia creation on chassis no 0473 SA which looked just as if it had come from Detroit with wrap-around glass, big fins and much chrome.

Mention must be also made of the first Superfast shown by Pinin Farina at the Paris Salon

Opposite: Ferrari Superamerica Series III 1959. One of 12 bodied by Pinin Farina. Above: Rear view of the same 410 Superamerica. Right: Sumptuous interior of 410 Superamerica.

of 1956. This was the forerunner to the 410 SA Series II with a 2600mm (8ft 6in) wheelbase. Only six of these were made before the third version of the 410 SA appeared again at Paris in 1958. The Series III was different in that it was the first Ferrari V12 to have its spark plugs on the outside of the cylinder heads nestling between the invariably hot exhaust manifolds. Dual distributors were fitted at the back of the engine and three Weber 42 DCF carburettors supplied the mixture. The power was up to 400bhp at 6500rpm and no less than eight final drive ratios were included in the specification in the brochure. The brochure, by the way, had no picture of the car in it! The 410 SA was the last Ferrari to be fitted with the Aurelio Lampredi V12 engine.

SPECIFICATION	410 SERIES I	SERIES II	SERIES III
ENGINE	V12, 4962cc	V12, 4962cc	V12, 4962 cc
HORSEPOWER	340bhp @ 6000rpm	380bhp @ 6500rpm	400bhp @ 6500rpm
TRANSMISSION	Manual 4-speed	Manual 4-speed	Manual 4-speed
CHASSIS	Steel tubular	Steel tubular	Steel tubular
SUSPENSION	Independent front, rigid rear axle (*all models*)		
BRAKES	Drum	Drum	Drum
TOP SPEED	261km/h (162mph)	261km/h (162mph)	266km/h (165mph)
ACCELERATION	0-96km/h (60mph): N/A	5.6sec	6.6sec
	0-161km/h (100mph): N/A	12.1sec	14.5sec

Production figures	In production	Total produced
Series I	1956	17
Series II	1957	6
Series III	1958-59	12

Ferrari 250 GT PF Coupé & Cabriolet

THE FERRARI factory by now had three distinct types of product – racing cars, berlinettas and 'road cars'. The racing cars, both single and two-seater sports racers, were always closest to Enzo Ferrari's heart. Even if he did not go to the races, he lived very much for their next victory. The berlinettas were looked after for their sportsman owners by the Assistenza Cliente department, which was run for a long time by Ing Florini.

Ing Florini would go to all the big races where the works sports racers were present as well, but he would be there to give help to the Concessionaire teams such Chinetti's North American Racing Team (NART), Ecurie Francorchamps, Jacque Swaters'

Belgian team and Colonel Ronnie Hoare's Maranello Concessionaires, as well as private owners who probably needed his help more than the others. The impetus for the road car production was probably stimulated by the coachbuilder as much as anyone – not to mention the clients.

The Paris Salon of 1958 saw the introduction of Pininfarina's elegant, if a little staid, 250 GT coupé. The cabriolet version had preceded the coupé in a rare reversal of events some months earlier. Automobile Ferrari had by now a worldwide dealer network and was represented in 17 countries by 41 dealers including 12 in Italy alone. Cars had to be made to satisfy this growing family. Most of the concessionaires were owned or run by racing drivers

or enthusiasts who at the time were the only people who knew about Ferrari and really cared that they were looked after properly.

The 250 GT PF coupé and cabriolet were both very much evolutions from the preceding Boano-built cars with a steel tubular chassis, still with drum brakes and Houdaille shock absorbers. The V12 3 litre Colombo engine started out with one distributor but gained another a year later – this mainly in the interests of reliability. Setting up distributors and ignition timing was as crucial to first class performance as the ability to balance six or more carburettors. In the late '50s there were no electronic systems to ensure correct settings and so the old tales about having to have a mechanic in the boot of a Ferrari were not totally unfounded.

Creature comforts came to the fore in the new Pininfarina design and heating and ventilation, comfortable seats with adjustment for rake, and generous luggage accommodation were more important in the brochure than pictures of the chassis and suspension. By 1959 the cabriolet version, which was to remain in production until 1962, looked very much like an open version of the coupé with the same details to front and rear. A factory hard top made the cabriolet look even more like the coupé, and indeed the cabriolet with hard top made the coupé obsolete. It continued in

Left: 250 GT Pininfarina Coupé. This elegant shape looks good in light metallic colours.

SPECIFICATION	250 GT PF COUPE
ENGINE	V12, 2953cc
HORSEPOWER	240bhp @ 7000rpm
TRANSMISSION	Manual 4-speed
CHASSIS	Steel tubular
SUSPENSION	Independent front, rigid rear axle
BRAKES	Drum until 1960, then discs
TOP SPEED	203km/h (126mph)
ACCELERATION	0-96km/h (60mph): 7.1sec
	0-161km/h (100mph): 17.5sec

production for two more years. By 1960, 350 coupés had been built by Pininfarina, which was many more than any other Ferrari so far. The later cabriolets had outside-plug engines, telescopic shock absorbers and disc brakes.

Production figures	In production	Total produced
250 GT PF coupé	1958-60	350
250 GT PF cabriolet I	1957-59	41
250 GT PF cabriolet II	1959-62	200

Left: Ferrari 250 GT Pininfarina Cabriolet Series II, chassis # 2327 GT. The cabriolet cockpit was dominated by the wood-trimmed alloy steering wheel. This example has a 'wireless' in front of the gear lever.

Above: The same car, chassis # 2327 GT, sporting an appropriate registration number. The coachwork is rather heavy and over-luxurious for a true cabriolet with styling that looks very much like an open version of the coupé.

Ferrari 250 GT SWB & 250 GT California

THE FIRST steel-bodied 250 GT, commonly referred to as the Short Wheel Base version, was chassis no 1993. It was delivered on 28th July, l960, to Colonel Ronnie Hoare of Maranello Concessionaires in the UK. It was blue and right-hand-drive. The lightweight competition version was first seen at the Paris Show in October l959.

This glorious car was designed by Pininfarina and built in either steel or aluminium by Scaglietti in Modena. They shared a similar chassis on a 2400mm (7ft 10in) wheelbase and used Colombo's V12. The FIA, (*Federation International de l'Automobile*), motor sport's governing body both then and now, granted homologation rights in appendix J of the International Sporting Code to the new 250 SWB on 16th June 1960. The street specification included a pair of distributors, each with two sets of points and 12 spark plugs on the outside of the V. The new cylinder heads also had new inlet ports, this time there was one per cylinder which was a development that derived from the racing engine fitted to the 250 TR. It had a 4-speed gearbox with an alloy case and a single dry plate clutch. Disc brakes were fitted front and rear together with Borani wire wheels with alloy rims of either 15 or 16 inch diameter (38.1 or 40.6cm), 5½ or 6 inches (14 or 15.2cm) wide. The road car usually had a Pirelli Cinturato and the racer almost universally a Dunlop R5 racing tyre.

The 250 brochure lists seven available final drive ratios which really means that this car could win from Brands Hatch to Le Mans – the maximum speed at 7000rpm being from 203km/h (126mph) with the lowest 7/32 ratio up to 269km/h (167mph) with the highest. The alloy-cased differential in which these gears were housed was connected via a rubber 'doughnut' coupling and a short propeller shaft to a ribbed all-alloy gearbox (in the case of a lightweight competition car) and an unribbed case for the steel-bodied car. The three Weber 40DCZ carburettors were fitted with a large air cleaner whilst the racer could have three double-choke Weber 40 DCZs with bare trumpets noisily sucking in air. The superb lines of the SWB, which looks great from any angle, are only matched by the handling. The superb balance urging the driver to push harder allows the adhesion both front and rear to flow gently into a beautiful drift. As always with

a Ferrari, the straight line stability just seems to improve the faster you go. The comfort afforded by the excellent suspension with good shock absorbers also means a bit of roll when the car is pressed, though this is probably more noticeable to the spectator than the driver.

The 250 GT Short Wheel Base California was one of the best-looking open cars ever made by Ferrari, easy on the eye and with more performance than open air motoring actually requires. This again was constructed by Scaglietti in Modena in two types. The first one generally had normal headlamps while the last ones had perspex covers. Some of the 250 SWB Californias competed seriously but none as successfully as the earlier LWB cars. The body material of the 250 California was steel or aluminium and either material could be chosen at the time of ordering. One can only assume that steel cars were offered at all because their wings did not flex when sat on!

The competition record of the 250 SWB is legendary with perhaps the most memorable triumph being Stirling Moss winning the Tourist Trophy at Goodwood in August 1960. Nearly every important International GT event in 1960 was won by a Ferrari 250 SWB from the 1000km of Buenos Aires in January to the 1000km of Paris at Monthléry in October.

Production figures	In production	Total produced
250 GT SWB	1960-62	167
250 GT SWB California	1960-63	55

Below: Ferrari 250 GT Short Wheel Base, chassis # 1993 GT. This actual car was the first Ferrari imported by Maranello Concessionaires in 1960. The steel body was made by Scaglietti in Modena.

Left and far left: Ferrari 250 GT California, chassis # 3021. This is a fine example of Scaglietti's superbly styled Short Wheel Base California, featuring the air intake on the bonnet, twin spot lights, perspex covers to the headlamps, and wraparound bumpers.

SPECIFICATION	250 GT SWB	250 GT SWB CALIFORNIA
ENGINE	V12, 2953cc	V12, 2953cc
HORSEPOWER	240/280bhp @ 7000rpm	280bhp @ 7000rpm
TRANSMISSION	Manual 4-speed	Manual 4-speed
CHASSIS	Steel tubular	Steel tubular
SUSPENSION	Independent front, rigid rear axle *(both models)*	
BRAKES	Disc	Disc
TOP SPEED	241km/h (150mph)	233km/h (145mph)
ACCELERATION	0-96km/h (60mph): 5.9sec 0-161km/h (100mph): 13.2sec	N/A N/A

25

Ferrari 250 GTE 2+2 & 330 America

HOW DO you make a true four-seater on the same wheelbase as the previous two-seater model? Together Ferrari and Pininfarina came up with the first true four-seat Ferrari, the 250 GTE, cleverly thought out and beautifully balanced – a most admirable Ferrari indeed. The chassis was inherited from the 250 GT Pininfarina coupé and modified to accept the engine some 200mm (8in) further forward. The factory designation was a type 508E chassis – hence the epithet E in GTE. The suspension used wishbones, coil springs and telescopic dampers at the front and semi-elliptics with twin radius arms and telescopic dampers at the rear. Dunlop disc brakes with a servo all round and Borani wire wheels with three eared 'knock offs' completed the chassis.

The Colombo V12 was fitted with three double-choke Weber 40 DCL/6 carburettors and had outside plugs like the 250 GT Pininfarina Coupé. A 4-speed gearbox was used in conjunction with an electrically operated overdrive, or step-up ratio, which improved fuel economy at high speed and reduced engine revolutions by 22 per cent. It only worked in 4th gear and was not considered a success. The coachwork by Pininfarina was developed closely with Ferrari and was the result of wind-tunnel testing which in 1960 was very avant-garde. The heating and cold air ventilation systems were carefully considered, and grilles were fitted on each side of the engine compartment to allow hot air out. The maximum use of space enabled a good-sized boot to be found at the back of the car. Four large chrome tail pipes protruded from beneath the wrap-around rear bumper. In the front, two driving lights were recessed into the corners of the typical Ferrari 'egg crate' grille. A beautiful polished aluminium prancing horse emblem was fixed to this grille just below the bonnet badge.

The 250 GTE handled beautifully and had the excellent balance of its two-seat predecessors.

The importance of this new car to Ferrari was that it reached new markets where two-seaters were not considered practical. Nearly a car a day was made for three years, which was a high production rate for Ferrari, and there were very few changes in specification or special bodies built, which speaks well for the initial design. The new car's baptism was surely masterminded by a shrewd marketing man as a prototype was provided for the Clerk of the Course in June 1960, at Les Vingt Quartre Heures du Mans. This was the first time the new 2+2 had been seen by the assembled world motoring press, and the racers and berlinettas did the new occasion proud by taking six of the seven top places. Its more conventional next appearance was at the Paris Salon later in the year. Towards the end of 1963 production ceased, but not before some 50 cars had been built with a new 4 litre V12 engine. The 330 America, as this version was called, was otherwise identical to the 250 and all were sold in North America. This was the stop-gap car before the 330 GT 2+2 appeared – more of which later.

Production figures	In production	Total produced
250 GTE 2+2	1960-63	950
330 America	1963	50

SPECIFICATION	250 GTE 2+2	330 AMERICA
ENGINE	V12, 2953cc	V12, 3967cc
HORSEPOWER	235bhp @ 7000rpm	300bhp @ 6600rpm
TRANSMISSION	Manual 4-speed + OD	Manual 4-speed + OD
CHASSIS	Steel tubular	Steel tubular
SUSPENSION	Independent front, rigid rear axle *(both models)*	
BRAKES	Disc	Disc
TOP SPEED	219km/h (136mph)	245km/h (152mph)
ACCELERATION	0-96km/h (60mph): 7.5sec	6.3sec
	0-161km/h (100mph): 18.2sec	N/A

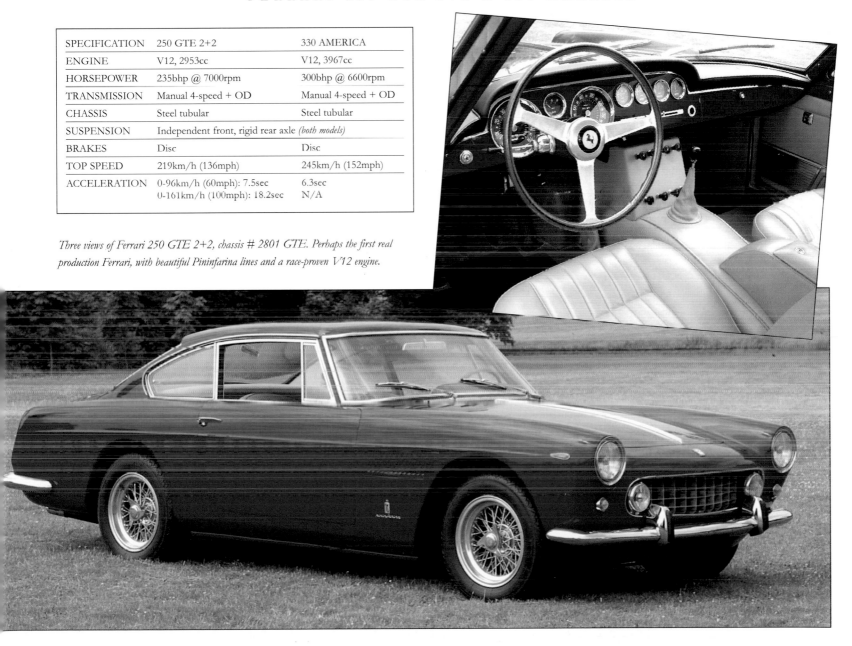

Three views of Ferrari 250 GTE 2+2, chassis # 2801 GTE. Perhaps the first real production Ferrari, with beautiful Pininfarina lines and a race-proven V12 engine.

27

Ferrari 400 Superamerica

FERRARI WAS by this time a thriving car factory producing almost a car a day. Most of these were 250 variants, but for the seriously rich the bespoke was available in the shape of the 400SA. This was the first car to be called by a number that did not represent the cubic capacity of the single cylinder. The four litre engine should, by rights, have led to the title 330 but no – 400 it was to be.

The Colombo design formed the basis of this engine and it featured outside plugs, and three Weber 42 DCN carburettors. This car succeeded the 410 SA, so comparisons are obvious. The 400 engine was physically smaller and the chassis shorter in wheelbase at 2420mm (7ft 11in). Word of mouth basically sold this car, as no brochure was produced,

despite some delightful contemporary Pininfarina photographs being taken. The chassis conformed to the regular specification of an early '60s Ferrari with oval steel tubes, wishbone front suspension with coil springs and telescopic dampers, whilst at the rear a rigid axle was suspended on semi-elliptical springs. Disc brakes brought the heavy – 1588kg (3500lb) – car to a stop. A single plate clutch drove a 4-speed gearbox to which was fitted a Laycock de Normanville overdrive unit.

The first 400 SA Pininfarina cabriolet was shown at the Brussels Show in 1960, while a coupé had been shown at Turin earlier. Each motor show until 1963 featured a 400 SA of some description on the Ferrari stand – it must truly have been one of those cars that people just stare at for hours. Pininfarina clothed all but two of the 400 SA with magnificent examples of the coachbuilder's art, all slightly different from one another, and all the coupés had long flowing powerful lines.

Chassis no 2207 SA was the personal car of Battista Pinin Farina and was first seen at the Turin

Below: Ferrari 400 Superamerica coupé by Pininfarina.

28

Left: Ferrari 400 Superamerica coupé showing the aerodynamic styling of this powerful grand tourer.

29

Show in 1960 titled SuperFast II. This car had its bodywork reworked several times becoming SuperFast III and IV. The later 400 SAs had their wheelbases lengthened to 2600mm (8ft 6in) in order to give the occupants more room.

There is no question that 400 SAs were the last really extravagant 'haute couture' examples of carrozzeria. So few were made that a dealer would not have had one in stock. They were the contemporary equivalent of a 288 GTO or an F40.

The only people likely to own one would be loyal clients of some years standing. I suggest that Pininfarina knew that the days of 'one offs' would shortly disappear for ever and that he looked upon the 400 SA as an opportunity to create his masterpieces before it was too late.

Production figures	In production	Total produced
Series I	1960-62	coupé 19/cab 6
Series II	1963-64	coupé 19/cab 3

SPECIFICATION	400 SA SERIES I & II
ENGINE	V12, 3967cc
HORSEPOWER	340bhp @ 7000rpm
TRANSMISSION	Manual 4-speed + OD
CHASSIS	Steel tubular
SUSPENSION	Independent front, rigid rear axle
BRAKES	Disc
TOP SPEED	265km/h (165mph)
ACCELERATION	N/A

Ferrari 250 GT Berlinetta Lusso

THE PARIS Salon in October 1962 saw the debut of many people's favourite Ferrari, the 250 GT Berlinetta Lusso. The 250 SWB, along with its look-alike road car, was superseded and the Lusso became the luxury two-seater coupé in Ferrari's line-up.

The chassis, with a wheelbase of 2400mm (7ft 10 1/2in), the same as the Lusso's new stablemate the 250 GTO, was made of oval-section steel tube in the best Ferrari manner. The front suspension was by forged steel wishbones, coil springs and Koni telescopic dampers. The rear axle was located with twin radius arms, semi-elliptical leaf springs on each side and a Watts linkage. The Watts linkage pivoted on the rear of the differential housing and by means of two arms prevented the axle from moving sideways. The rear dampers were surrounded by light springs which assisted the system. Ferrari were thus typically conservative in retaining both springing mediums, before opting for coil springs only on later models. Servo-assisted disc brakes and Borrani wire wheels completed the chassis.

The 3 litre V12 engine had a compression ratio of 9.2:1 with the normal Ferrari arrangement of an overhead cam per bank operating inclined valves via roller rockers. The engine was slightly further forward in the frame than that of the 250 GTO and did not have dry sump lubrication. Three Weber 36 DCS carburettors were fitted to most Lussos under a black-painted air filter that spanned all three units. Twin Marelli distributors and a pair of oil filters were also readily apparent when the bonnet was opened.

SPECIFICATION	250 GT LUSSO
ENGINE	V12, 2953cc
HORSEPOWER	250bhp @ 7000rpm
TRANSMISSION	Manual 4-speed
CHASSIS	Steel tubular
SUSPENSION	Independent front, rigid rear axle
BRAKES	Disc
TOP SPEED	240km/h (149mph)
ACCELERATION	0-96km/h (60mph): 8sec 0-161km/h (100mph): 19.5sec

The bodywork designed by Pininfarina was subcontracted to Scaglietti in Modena, who used steel for most of the fixed panels and skinned the doors and lids in aluminium. Most northern European examples have suffered badly from rust. The boot was small, but additional luggage space was available behind the seats, the spare wheel being in the boot. The coachwork achieved that classic Ferrari feeling of motion when standing still, and is the distillation of all that Ferrari and Farina had done before. The truncated Kamm tail appeared on the Lusso for the first time; it is an aerodynamic feature to be found on many succeeding Ferrari cars. Plain circular rear lights sourced locally were also to be seen again. The egg crate grille sloped forward eagerly between headlights on the tips of the wings. Generous glass area made visibility particularly good, although some drivers find the big wood-rimmed steering wheel set too high. The

Left and right: Ferrari 250 GT Berlinetta Lusso, chassis # 4655 GT. Two pictures of the same car showing Scaglietti's interpretation of Pininfarina's fine design.

speedometer and rev counter were mounted in the centre of the dash, oddly angled towards the driver.

The non-adjustable bucket seats gave reasonable support and the first seat-belts fitted to Ferrari were also in evidence – albeit they were optional. One more Motor Show and the Ferrari 250 becomes history. The 250 Colombo engine, which had lasted from Bracco's Mille Miglia of 1952 to Lusso chassis no. 5955GT, had truly left its mark in lists of race winners, wonderful touring cars and the unforgettable scream of twelve cylinders down the Mulsanne Straight at Le Mans.

Production figures	In production	Total produced
250 GT Lusso	1962-64	350

Right: Lusso interior showing the unique placing of speedometer and rev counter angled towards the driver.

Ferrari 330 GT 2+2

Ferrari 330 GT 2+2 Series I, chassis # 6497. Three good pictures of a four-headlamp Series I example, despite non-standard wing mirrors and the wrong gear lever knob!

IN EARLY 1964 at the Brussels Show the 330 GT 2+2 made its first public appearance. As a successor to the 330 America, the new car had an entirely new body and a longer chassis.

The engine was similar to the 400 SA in capacity but differed in details such as bore centre measurements and engine mounts. Up until now all Ferrari engine mounts had consisted of four cast lugs on the engine block which housed rubber bushes. These lugs sat on raised brackets welded to the base tubes of the chassis. The 330 GT 2+2 Mark I had a 4-speed gearbox with a single dry plate clutch in unit with the engine. At the back of the gearbox was fitted a Laycock de Normanville electrically operated overdrive unit. This was in effect the 5th gear and only worked when the mechanical gearbox was in top. The well-spaced ratios all had synchromesh. A one-piece prop shaft with universal joints and a sliding spline took the drive from gearbox to axle which was located by semi-elliptical leaf springs and two radius arms each side. Telescopic shock absorbers were mounted concentrically with small coil springs above the axle. There was only one ratio available as it was most unlikely that anyone would use a 2+2 for competition. The 8/34 ratio was good for 245km/h (152mph) at 6400rpm in overdrive.

The front suspension as usual used forged wishbones all mounted on beautifully engineered pins and bushes. The coil springs were attached to the lower wishbones via a swinging cup structure so

that the spring was never bent and an anti-roll bar mounted in rubber bushes helped handling. The telescopic shock absorbers were mounted between the top wishbones and a bracket which protruded into the engine bay. They were adjustable and it was therefore possible to choose how stiff you wanted the ride to be. The 330 had a large turning circle of 13.7m (45ft). Turning was controlled by a worm and peg steering box operating track rods via an idler arm and a central tie-rod. The four-wheel disc brake system was operated via a double master cylinder, two servos and two reservoirs as two separate systems to front

and rear brakes. Braking distance in ideal conditions from 161km/h (100mph) was 114m (375ft).

The bodywork was that of a genuine four-seater with quite generous luggage space. The cabin felt spacious and the driver's view was excellent. The four headlamps may not have pleased everyone but

SPECIFICATION	330 GT 2+2 SERIES I	SERIES II
ENGINE	V12, 3967cc	V12, 3967cc
HORSEPOWER	300bhp @ 6600rpm	300bhp @ 6600rpm
TRANSMISSION	Manual 4-speed + OD	Manual 5-speed
CHASSIS	Steel tubular	Steel tubular
SUSPENSION	Independent front, rigid rear axle *(both models)*	
BRAKES	Disc	Disc
TOP SPEED	245km/h (152mph)	245km/h (152mph)
ACCELERATION	0-96km/h (60mph): 8sec	8sec

33

they certainly lit the road ahead. The 330 made a glorious twelve cylinder noise and was always a great pleasure to drive – maybe because one could share it with two or three friends.

The 330 sold well, which reinforced the point that the model line-up needed a 2+2. During 1965 the Mark II appeared with a new nose incorporating only two headlights and different hot air vents behind the front wheels. Alloy wheels were optional for the first time on a 2+2 and a new 5-speed gearbox replaced the sometimes temperamental overdrive and 4-speed gearbox. It is probable that the last 330 GT 2+2s had the new engine mounts which appeared on the 330 GTC and 275 GTB/4.

Production figures	In production	Total produced
Series I	1964-65	500
Series II	1965-66	575

Ferrari 275 GTB & 275 GTS

AT THE Paris Salon of 1964 Ferrari unveiled a beautiful new berlinetta and a brand new spider – respectively the 275 GTB and GTS. These two glorious cars shared the same new chassis and engine. Both bodies were designed by Pininfarina and were to be made by Scaglietti in Modena.

The Colombo V12 from the Lusso was bored out a further 25cc per cylinder giving a capacity of 3.3 litres. The new 5-speed gearbox was in unit with the differential at the back of the car. The open drive shaft, steadied by a central chassis-mounted bearing, joined the clutch, still on the back of the engine, to the new transmission. The gear selection rod went forward between the seats to a gear lever mounted in the conventional position. The correct shimming of the central drive-line bearing was crucial to smooth running, and the transmission was mounted on the chassis via three rubber bushes. The next element in the specification of both GTB and GTS was a first for Ferrari – they had independent rear suspension. This was achieved with double pressed steel wishbones, concentric coil springs and adjustable shock absorbers. An anti-roll bar was actuated from the lower wishbones and from either side of the limited slip differential, universally jointed sliding spline shafts drove the rear wheels. The original brochure for the 275 GTB mentions rack and pinion steering but this was premature – the 275 retained the familiar worm and peg ZF steering box.

A choice could be made when ordering a 275 GTB between a steel and aluminium body, three or six pairs of Weber carburettors and alloy or wire wheels. At Le Mans in 1965 a 275 GTB came 3rd overall driven by Willie Mairesse and 'Beurlys', for Ecurie Francorchamps, and the following year Roy Pike and Piers Courage came 8th overall for Ronnie Hoare's team in chassis no. 09035 GT. The amazing versatility of Ferrari's racing road cars shines again.

Development of the 275 did not stand still and the fitting in 1966 of a torque tube between the clutch housing and transmission was a very welcome addition. The engine block was modified to have only one engine mount each side and the

Left: Ferrari 275 GTB, chassis # 7715 GT. This is an early shortnose car with optional Borani wire wheels.

Below: Ferrari 275 GTS, chassis # 6989 GT, pictured in front of Maranello Concessionaires' building in Egham. This example has an extra wide passenger seat which effectively makes it a three-seater.

SPECIFICATION	275 GTB	275 GTS
ENGINE	V12, 3285cc	V12, 3285cc
HORSEPOWER	300bhp @ 7500rpm (6 carbs)	260bhp @ 7000rpm
TRANSMISSION	Manual 5-speed	Manual 5-speed
CHASSIS	Steel tubular	Steel tubular
SUSPENSION	Independent all round *(both models)*	
BRAKES	Disc	Disc
TOP SPEED	257km/h (160mph) (6 carbs)	233km/h (145mph)
ACCELERATION	0-96km/h (60mph): 6.5sec	7.2sec
	0-161km/h (100mph): N/A	18.8sec

torque tube had flanges at each end which joined the engine and transmission in one solid unit. The gearbox now only had two mounts. This all made for a much smoother delivery of power and also made gear selection easier. Straight-line stability was improved with a longer, lower front to the already streamlined nose and rearward visibility improved with a larger rear window. This necessitated putting the boot hinges on the outside. In the interests of a smooth line the petrol filler cap was housed inside the rear luggage compartment as was the spare wheel. This left a smallish boot but there was good space behind the seats. The 275 was one of the first Ferraris to hang the clutch and brake pedals from above rather than pivoting on the floor. The single overhead camshafts per bank operated inclined valves via roller rockers and were driven by a triple roller chain.

The 275 GTS, although sharing all the mechanical details, never seemed as glamorous as the GTB, particularly when fitted with its optional hard top.

Production figures	In production	Total produced
275 GTB	1964-66	456
275 GTS	1964-66	200

Below: Ferrari 275 GTB, chassis # 08647 GT. The cockpit features white-on-black instrument faces and black-topped gear lever in its exposed gate. Bottom: Rear view of same car with familiar round tail lights and four exhaust pipes.

Below: 3.3-litres of Ferrari V12 engine, topped by six double-choke Weber carburettors. Right: The 'longnose' GTB in all its glory. Note the alloy knock-off wheels with ten holes around the centre on this car.

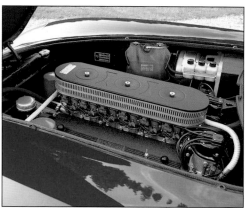

Ferrari 275 GTB/4 & NART Spider

MAURO Forgheri, still in his early days at Ferrari, designed the four-camshaft cylinder heads for the 275 P2 of 1965. This sports racer was a development of the 250 P but was new for the '65 season, at the beginning of which Nino Vaccarella and Lorenzo Bandini won the 49th Targa Florio. The four-overhead-camshaft cylinder heads were to appear, in traditional Ferrari fashion passing from racer to roadcar, at the Paris Salon of 1966 when the new 275 GTB/4 was introduced.

The 275 GTB was the epitome of what everyone thought a Ferrari should look like, and by 1966 it had been developed into a luxurious, mechanically refined and successful Grand Touring car. All the best features like the torque tube and the longer nose were retained, but the most exciting element was under the bonnet where 300bhp at 8000rpm was achieved with the new cylinder heads and four cams. The engine could have been lowered in the chassis as a dry sump lubrication system had

been adopted, but no – the taller engine required a smooth blister on the bonnet which distinguished the four cam from its predecessor. The oil tank was mounted to one side within the engine compartment. In the four cam brochure the car was shown with alloy wheels, a fairly plain design with ten small holes around the rim. These, of course, were a production 'look-alike' of the current Ferrari racing wheel. Wire wheels and a steel or alloy body were offered as options when a new car was purchased.

SPECIFICATION	275 GTB/4	275 GTB/4 NART SPIDER
ENGINE	V12, 3285cc	V12, 3285cc
HORSEPOWER	300bhp @ 8000rpm	300bhp @ 8000rpm
TRANSMISSION	Manual 5-speed	Manual 5-speed
CHASSIS	Steel tubular	Steel tubular
SUSPENSION	Independent all round (both models)	
BRAKES	Disc	Disc
TOP SPEED	267km/h (166mph)	249km/h (155mph)
ACCELERATION	0-96km/h (60mph): N/A 0-161km/h (100mph): N/A	6.7sec 15sec

Below: Ferrari 275 GTB/4, chassis # 10843 GT. A gorgeous silver example showing its Kamm tail and nearly horizontal rear window, all indistinguishable from a late two cam.

There is no doubt that at the time the four cam was the pinnacle of automotive achievement, certainly without equal in the realm of exciting engine noises. It begged to be revved and provided great excitement on a clear road, whether straight or twisty. Care was needed, as with all machines, until the oil and water had warmed up when the gearbox was a joy to use. Together with the responsiveness of the throttle, this engine established the feeling of awe in which this car is now held.

Built on the same 2400mm (7ft 10½in) chassis and using all the same mechanicals, Luigi Chinetti commissioned a spider version of the four cam. The North American dealer saw that a really sporting open car was needed to fill the gap left by the Californias, and Scaglietti built 10 examples now known as NART spiders. The chassis and mechanicals were unchanged and what a beautiful job Scaglietti did. It seems a pity that the commission had not been undertaken sooner and in greater numbers, but it must not be forgotten that it was a hard job selling Ferraris in the '60s and a more desirable version was one way of 'moving the metal'. The four cam was in production for just over a year and few serious attempts at competition were tried.

Production figures	In production	Total produced
275 GTB/4	1966-68	350
NART spider	1967	10

Left: The four cam beautifully presented its subtle swelling on the bonnet; the only tell-tale sign that it is not a longnose two cam. Right: Ferrari 275 GTB/4, chassis # 11019, in action.

Ferrari 330, 365 GTC & GTS

FERRARI always built more coupés than spiders of any model and the 330 and 365 GTC are no exception. The 330 GTC débuted at Geneva in 1966. Designed and built by Pininfarina, this car was really a replacement for the Lusso. It was built on the traditional steel tube chassis of 2400mm (7ft 10 1/2in) wheelbase with the four litre V12 from the 2+2, but now with two engine mounts and a torque tube connecting it to the 5-speed transaxle mounted between the rear wheels. Light alloy wheels of the '10 small holes' variety, servo-assisted disc brakes, all-round wishbone suspension, and the familiar worm and roller steering contributed to making a fine handling, well balanced car.

The lines of the GTC were not unlike the 330 GT 2+2 MkII with a shorter wheelbase. The view from inside was unrestricted and the cabinet felt spacious. The rear-mounted transmission was controlled by a lever working within the chromed confines of the traditional Ferrari gate – obstinate when cold, and noisy when warm as it is smacked from one finger to another.

Electric windows were a newish innovation for Ferrari and a certain mistrust in their reliability was evidenced by the supply of a crank handle (usually in the glove box) which could manually raise a window glass. The little leather covers for the crank holes never went back into place as they were meant to. Air conditioning was an optional extra, probably standard in America but not yet thought of as essential in Europe.

Carrozzeria Pininfarina issued a press release at the 54th Paris Motor Show of October 1967 on the cars which it had designed. Part of the release concerning the 330 GTC states: 'The fuel cap, made of a light alloy with the famous Ferrari horse in the centre, is controlled from the inside by a lever, which can be reached from the driving seat. In this way refuelling is possible without getting down from the car'. How times have changed!

The four litre engine had three Weber 40 DCZ/6 double-choke carburettors which were fed by an army of pumps, both electric Bendix and FISPA, and a mechanical pump driven off the bottom of the front timing cover. Two distributors each with two pairs of points supplied two coils and

SPECIFICATION	330	365
ENGINE	V12, 3967cc	V12, 4390cc
HORSEPOWER	300bhp @ 6600rpm	320bhp @ 6600rpm
TRANSMISSION	Manual 5-speed	Manual 5-speed
CHASSIS	Steel tubular	Steel tubular
SUSPENSION	Independent all round (both models)	
BRAKES	Disc	Disc
TOP SPEED	243km/h (151mph)	243km/h (151mph)
ACCELERATION	0-96km/h (60mph): 6.9sec	N/A

Left: 365 GTC, chassis # 12557 GT, being exercised at the old Goodwood Motor Racing Circuit. Note the clean flanks.

twelve spark plugs. The servo assisted disc brakes had a tandem master cylinder and separate systems back and front. The seats were adjustable fore and aft and also for rake. Together with adjustable pads on the brake and clutch pedal this made for a comfortable driving position. Ferrari supplied very comprehensive tool kits for his cars from the early days and the 330 GTC had a heavy brown leatherette bag containing 25 items including a lead hammer for removing wheels, a grease gun, hub pullers and more familiar things like spanners.

At Earls Court in October 1966 the 330 GTS was first seen in London. This was a spider version of the GTC and it shared all the same mechanicals. The Earls Court 330 GTS chassis no 09155 was finished in white. The first right-hand-drive 365 GTC chassis no. 12107 was collected from Modena in February 1969. This handsome car was painted Grigio Mahmoud, a dark metallic silver. Life has been kind to it and it still has it original paint. The 365 had a 4.4 litre V12 engine and was distinguished by air exit vents on the engine lid and smooth flanks, unlike the 330 which had three vent louvres above the Pininfarina badge. A spider version the 365 GTS was also made in very limited numbers. The last rhd 365 GTC was collected from Modena in May 1970.

Above: Ferrari 330 GTC, chassis # 9317 GT. Almost identical to the 365 except for the air vents behind the front wheels. Below: Ferrari 365 GTS, chassis # 12457.

Production figures	In production	Total produced
330	1966-68	600 GTC/100 GTS
365	1968-70	150 GTC/20 GTS

Ferrari 500 Superfast & 365 California

THE FERRARI Superfast made its debut at the Geneva Show of 1964 and was first seen at Earls Court on Pininfarina's stand in October of the same year. This very special car was by far and away the most expensive car at the show – it cost over 20 per cent more that a Rolls Royce Phantom V limousine!

The 500 Superfast used a unique 5 litre engine of Lampredi dimensions but Colombo features.

The '64 Earls Court show car was chassis no. 6345 and was delivered to the client by Maranello Concessionaires' chairman Colonel Ronnie Hoare more or less the day after the show. In the original order schedule this car was referred to as a 5 litre Superamerica coupé which indicates that although the concessionaire knew that a special model was coming the factory had not by then decided what to call it.

The 500 Superfast's chassis' main dimensions were the same as the 330 GT 2+2. Front suspension was independent with wishbones, coil springs, telescopic dampers and an anti-roll bar. Rear suspension used a rigid axle suspended on semi-elliptical springs together with twin radius arms. The 500 Superfast was one of the earliest Ferraris to be fitted with power-assisted steering which was beautifully weighted, as indeed it has been ever since.

and open body did not enhance body/chassis stiffness and the handling of the 365 California was not a strong point.

Production figures	In production	Total produced
500 Superfast	1964-66	36
365 California	1966-67	14

Opposite: Ferrari 500 Superfast, chassis # 6673: one of Pininfarina's masterpieces, both in terms of design and execution. Left: Ferrari 365 California with the pop-up lights on the nose in the closed position. Below: The 5-litre engine of 500 SF, chassis # 6673, well and truly filled the space.

This characteristic has prompted many people, when driving a Ferrari for the first time, to ask whether it has power steering or not. The early Superfasts had a 4-speed and overdrive gearbox but as with the 330, this became a new 5-speed gearbox, which was a better proposition altogether.

The long regal body was designed and made by Pininfarina in Turin and its antecedents can be distinguished from the 400 SA through the Superfast prototypes. The clean line, without over embellishment, gives an air of power and strength to this prestigious vehicle.

The 365 California was not in production at the same time as the 500 Superfast, but followed on from it as a quasi-successor to that model. Even fewer were made and it was produced for only a year. The chassis dimensions were the same as those of the 500 SF and 330 2+2, as were the suspension specifications. It is, however, the first time we hear of the '365' – an engine size which was to be popular with Ferrari for another ten years. In the

365 California the engine produced 320bhp at 6600rpm using three double-choke Weber 40 DF/1. After its introduction at Geneva in 1966, an example was shown by Pininfarina at Earls Court the same year but this was not destined to stay in England. The first of only two English clients had to wait until June 1967 before taking delivery of chassis no. 9985.

Pininfarina styling used a rear cooling duct which incorporated the door and rear wheel arch, an enduring feature which is still seen today in Ferrari's mid-engined cars. The pop-up spot lights, seen on the 365 California for the first time, anticipated minimum height for headlamp regulations and have been in use by Ferrari for the past 25 years. The long wheelbase

SPECIFICATION	500 SUPERFAST	365 CALIFORNIA
ENGINE	V12, 4963cc	V12, 4390cc
HORSEPOWER	400bhp @ 6500rpm	320bhp @ 6600rpm
TRANSMISSION	Manual 4-speed + OD, later 5-speed	Manual 5-speed
CHASSIS	Steel tubular	Steel tubular
SUSPENSION	Independent front, rigid rear axle *(both models)*	
BRAKES	Disc	Disc
TOP SPEED	282km/h (175mph)	246km/h (153mph)
ACCELERATION	N/A	N/A

43

Ferrari Dino 206 GT, 246 GT & GTS

VITTORIO Jano had worked with Enzo Ferrari at Alfa Romeo in the '30s and it was he who in 1955 introduced the V6 to Ferrari. It was Ferrari's engineer son Dino, who was by then terminally ill, who persuaded him to build the V6 which now bears his name. From Grand Prix cars through sports prototypes to a little jewel of a road car first seen at the Turin Show in 1967, the Dino 206 GT was born.

The aerodynamics were greatly influenced by Pininfarina's wind-tunnel testing and designs from the earlier sports prototypes. The execution as a road car was a triumph for all-round visibility which was considered to be so difficult a factor in the design of a mid-engined car. The 206 GT was built on a traditional steel tube chassis with double wishbone independent suspension all round, together with concentric springs and dampers. The alloy wheels were secured with three eared 'knock offs' and Pininfarina's body was entirely made of alloy. The V6 with four overhead camshafts was mounted transversely behind the driver and in front of the rear axle line. Power was taken from the clutch via drop gears to the transverse gearbox, which was in unit with the differential and engine sump.

The mechanical layout remained the same for all the V6 and V8 transverse-engined cars up to 1989. The 206 with its all-alloy body, leather seats, knock-off wheels and all-alloy engine was too expensive and did not sell well. At the Geneva Motor Show of 1969 the 246 GT was first shown to the public. The changes included plastic seats, an iron engine block, bolt-on wheels, a steel body, more power, better torque and a lower price. This was the recipe for success and by 1974 the Dino 246 GT and its spider version the 246 GTS had sold over 3500 examples. The GTS version was introduced in 1972 and shared the same mechanicals as the 246 GT. The spider version was not a true open car as the rear window and all its supports remained in position after the rigid panel (the roof) had been removed. This panel was then stowed vertically behind the seats. It could be extremely easily removed and replaced by one person.

Both versions were a revelation in terms of their roadholding and general stability. Nothing had been made like them before; handling was like that of a racing car. The Dino was also more user-friendly and reliable than the big V12s and was the first car from the Ferrari factory that could safely be kept as the owner's only car. Maximum power of 195bhp at 7600 rpm propelled the 246 to 241km/h (150mph). The feeling of supreme agility, excellent brakes which did not fade, and an engine and gearbox like a musical instrument, all urged the driver to go faster. Like the bigger V12s, the gear lever moved noisily between chromed fingers, and the leather rimmed steering wheel framed a black and yellow prancing horse horn button. The left foot could be rested on a properly designed footrest

Above: Ferrari Dino 206 GT, chassis # 0186. This fine example in Rosso Dino is pictured at Mugello in October 1995. Note the Knock-off wheels and exposed fuel filler cap, both identifying details of this little motoring gem.

to the left of the clutch. The rear view over the shoulders was excellent on the open road, though parking needed a little practice, particularly with such expensive corners.

Production figures	In production	Total produced
206 GT	1967-69	152
246 GT	1969-74	2487
246 GTS	1972-74	1274

SPECIFICATION	206 GT	246 GT	246 GTS
ENGINE	V6, 1986cc	V6, 2418cc	V6, 2418cc
HORSEPOWER	180bhp @ 8000rpm	195bhp @ 7600rpm	195bhp @ 7600rpm
TRANSMISSION	Manual 5-speed	Manual 5-speed	Manual 5-speed
CHASSIS	Steel tubular	Steel tubular	Steel tubular
SUSPENSION	Independent all round *(all models)*		
BRAKES	Disc	Disc	Disc
TOP SPEED	238km/h (148mph)	243km/h (151mph)	243km/h (151mph)
ACCELERATION	0-96km/h (60mph): 7.5sec 0-161km/h (100mph): N/A	6.8sec 18sec	6.8sec 18sec

45

Left: Ferrari Dino 246 GT. The small car that enabled Ferrari to offer a 'stepping stone' before buying a 12 cylinder. The 246 GT gave drivers the opportunity to experience the sort of handling and agility usually only possible in a racing car.

Below: Ferrari Dino 246 GTS. The spider version had a removable roof panel which stowed behind the seats. Both the Dino GTS and GT were easy to live with and reliable, making them suitable for everyday driving.

Ferrari 365 GT 2+2

ONCE AGAIN Ferrari chose Paris to unveil an important new car. This time it was the 365 GT 2+2. Pininfarina was entrusted with the coachwork and produced a generous 2+2 full of creature comforts, whilst retaining a good family likeness. The nose was low and streamlined, ending in an elliptical egg crate grille. The chrome half bumpers had side and turn lights set into the surface under very strong plastic lenses. The headlights were set back into the wings and in England usually had perspex covers. The large doors gave easy access to the rear seats. The rear quarter lights did not open, despite their large size, and the large, rather flat rear window had an electric demister. Six tail lights and four chrome exhaust pipes were separated by a full wrap-around rear bumper. The boot lid opened by means of a lever behind the driver's seat (lhd) to reveal the biggest boot so far for a Ferrari, under the floor of which were found the spare wheel and two fuel tanks.

The 4.4 litre engine came from the 365 California. It was attached to a magnificent 5-speed gearbox which, in turn, was attached to the chassis-mounted differential via a cast aluminium torque tube. The air conditioning compressor, the power-steering pump, water pump and the alternator were all driven off the front of the engine. The power steering fluid had its own small heat exchanger, and two Marelli distributors were driven from the back of the camshafts in the usual Ferrari way. The chassis had the same wheelbase, 2650mm (8ft 8in), as its predecessor, the 330 2+2, but used a wider track both front and rear. The new Michelin 200-VR

Below : Ferrari 365 GT 2+2. Its long, elegant lines gave ample interior space for driver and three passengers. This car is fitted with optional Borani wire wheels.

46

SPECIFICATION	365 2+2
ENGINE	V12, 4390cc
HORSEPOWER	320bhp @ 6600rpm
TRANSMISSION	Manual 5-speed
CHASSIS	Steel tubular
SUSPENSION	Independent all round
BRAKES	Disc
TOP SPEED	245km/h (152mph)
ACCELERATION	0-96km/h (60mph): 7.1sec
	0-161km/h (100mph): 15.7sec

15 tubeless tyres were a great success. They were usually fitted to the 'ten hole' alloy wheels although Borani wire wheels were still an option. The last 365 GT 2+2 made were fitted with five-spoke Daytona type wheels. Ventilated brake discs were fitted all-round and for the first time on a 2+2 the suspension was independent at the rear. This used the well proven system of double wishbones and concentric coil springs and shock absorbers. Alongside the suspension units were a pair of oleopneumatic struts which maintained the ride height at a constant level. These had been developed by Ferrari in conjunction with the Dutch firm Koni.

The big car was well equipped inside and together with speedometer, rev counter, oil pressure, water temperature and clock, there were to be found gauges for amps and engine oil temperature. On short journeys in winter it is rare to see the oil temperature gauge move. The early examples had electrically operated front quarter windows. These were later returned to manual control, but still by rotary motion. The air conditioning was complimented by a traditional

heating and fresh air system. The early 365 2+2s were the last Ferraris to have an electric pump which required switching on prior to starting and which had to be switched off once the engine was running properly. On the older cars it was always referred to as the 'Autoflux'.

Considering its size and weight the 365 went extremely well and felt safe and stable up to the maximum speed of over 241km/h (150mph). The engine was very docile and behaved well in traffic. Today one is tempted to say 'well so it jolly well should', but such sophistication was still new to Ferrari.

Above: Same 365 GT 2+2, the long tail offered reasonable luggage accommodation. Below: Interior of 365 GT 2+2 shows dashboard and electric window switches behind gear lever.

Production figures	In production	Total produced
365 2+2	1967-71	800

Ferrari 365 GTB4

THIS GREAT car is better known as 'the Daytona' – so called because of Ferrari's overwhelming victory in the Daytona continental 24 hours endurance race in Florida in January 1967. The first two places were taken by the legendary 330 P4 with a 412P in third place.

First seen at the Paris Salon in late 1968, it immediately established itself as the world's fastest car and, at 352bhp, amongst the most powerful. This was a real driver's car with excitement as a constant companion; few people can have mastered this true stallion without rolling their sleeves up. The Daytona was heavy and lumbering at any speed under 113km/h (70mph) but its real magic started to pump adrenalin from 161km/h (100mph)

48

onwards. It was road tested in excess of 274km/h (170mph) in 1971, and was a perfect example of Ferrari's incredible straight line stability giving confidence at very high speeds. Under the bonnet was a 60 degree four-cam V12 of 4.4 litres capacity using six down-draught, double-choke, Weber carburettors and dry sump lubrication. Power steering was considered unnecessary by Ferrari in such a sporting car, but many owners would have welcomed it. The engine drove the rear wheels via an engine-mounted clutch through a torque tube to a chassis-mounted transaxle which had five speeds. The steel tube chassis had independent suspension front and rear using double wishbones and concentric springs and dampers. Two hip-hugging

SPECIFICATION	365 GTB4 & S/4
ENGINE	V12, 4390cc
HORSEPOWER	352bhp @ 7500rpm
TRANSMISSION	Manual 5-speed
CHASSIS	Steel tubular
SUSPENSION	Independent all round
BRAKES	Disc
TOP SPEED	278km/h (173mph)
ACCELERATION	0-96km/h (60mph): 5.9sec 0-161km/h (100mph): 12sec

bucket seats covered with Connolly leather accommodated two people while there was a surprisingly generous amount of luggage space in the boot and behind the seats. This was a grand tourer in the truest sense, 800km (500 miles) in a day was strolling for this car anywhere in Europe.

The sweeping lines were designed by Pininfarina and built by Scaglietti in Modena. It was mostly fabricated in steel with aluminium used for the bonnet, boot and door skins. Headlights protected behind perspex screens added to the smooth nose of the early examples, though US regulations resulted in 'pop-up' headlights which have since been fitted to all but a few Ferraris.

The 365 GTS4 was an open spider version of the Daytona. This was not produced in great numbers and has since become much sought after by collectors. The closed car, as always, drives better than the spider.

Ferrari prepared 15 competition Daytonas from 1971-73. These were campaigned vigorously at international level until 1979 with many class successes at Le Mans and other endurance races.

In Ferrari's range of cars there is always 'a big berlinetta' – the yardstick car by which others are judged. The Daytona was the last such car to be front-engined.

Production figures	In production	Total produced
365 GTB4	1968-73	1284
S/4	1969-73	122

Opposite page: Ferrari 365 GTB4, chassis # 16713, fitted with a non standard chrome nose bar. Below: Although Ferrari built a number of 'Daytona Spiders' many, like this, were fabricated in the '80s by cutting the tops off coupés.

Ferrari 365 GTC4

INTRODUCED at the Paris Salon in October 1971 and seen in London for the first time two weeks later, the 365 GTC4 was a graceful Pininfarina design with clean almost sharp edges, and a black rubber front bumper that terminated the bonnet in a large elliptical shape. The 'C' was for coupé and the '4' for four camshafts.

This was not a mainstream Ferrari model but something between a berlinetta and a 2+2. The generous front seats were as usual trimmed in Connolly leather, but for early production GTC4s a range of tweed inserts were available. The rear seats too could be specified with tweed inserts and, though these only provided enough space for small children, they also folded down to reveal a well laid out platform on which luggage could be strapped. The centre console, through which the gear lever emerged, was finished in a plastic material resembling a 'kitchen top' which was very out of keeping with the rest of the interior. Many owners had this recovered in leather.

Built on a traditional Ferrari steel-tube chassis, with a steel body made in Turin by Pininfarina, the suspension was independent at back and front using double wishbones and concentric springs and shock absorbers. The rear suspension also used a Koni self-levelling device. Brakes both front and rear used ventilated discs; these were much less susceptible to fade than the Daytona. Power-assisted steering by ZF was precise and welcome.

The V12 engine at 4.4 litres shared crank and pistons with the Daytona, which had been in production for nearly three years by then, but it employed a wet sump and had different cylinder heads using six side-draught, double-choke Weber 38DCOE carburettors. The induction manifolds were incorporated in the inlet camshaft covers. This measure and the use of side-draught carburettors reduced the overall height of the engine, so enabling a lower bonnet line. This was a pure case of the stylists dictating to the engineers, although in this instance it resulted in a happy compromise. A 5-speed gearbox in unit with the engine was joined to the chassis-mounted differential by a substantial torque tube which drove the rear wheels.

There were no extras when the car was offered for sale. In fact it had a comprehensive specification for the time including air conditioning. Big Michelin radials on alloy rims were secured to the hubs with

Left: Ferrari 365 GTC4 showing tartan seat inserts and 'kitchen top' console. The bulk of the gearbox separates the driver from the passenger.

50

Above: Ferrari 365 GTC4, chassis # 15709. Right: 4.4-litres, wet sump and six side-draught, double-choke Webers.

SPECIFICATION	365 GTC4
ENGINE	60° V12, 4390cc
HORSEPOWER	330bhp @ 6200rpm
TRANSMISSION	Manual 5-speed
CHASSIS	Steel tubular
SUSPENSION	Independent all round
BRAKES	Disc
TOP SPEED	245km/h (152mph)
ACCELERATION	0-96km/h (60mph): 7.3sec 0-161km/h (100mph): 19.3sec

three eared steel 'knock offs'. It was at around this time that owners were becoming reluctant to swing a hammer at their beautiful cars, and legislators thought that 'knock off' nuts were a danger to pedestrians, so this was nearly the last Ferrari to be so equipped.

This was a magnificent car to drive and always inspired great confidence. It was a pity that the GTC4 was not developed further, as it would have complemented the very sporting 'Boxers' with its traditional values.

Production figures	In production	Total produced
365 GTC4	1971-72	500

Ferrari 365 GT4 2+2, 400, 400i & 412

FIRST SEEN at the Paris Salon in October 1972, this Pininfarina design was in some ways a stretched version of the 365 GTC4, the manufacture of which was discontinued more or less at the time that the 2+2 started. Four average-sized adults found adequate space inside but usually the 2+2's rear space was used for luggage or coats. This car had splendid visibility and generous head room for those in the back. The 118 litre (26 gallon) fuel tank would take you about 418km/h (260 miles) driven hard. It is, however, a heavy car. The 5-speed gearbox was in unit with the engine driving the rear wheels via a torque tube.

All-round independent suspension by double wishbones, concentric coil springs and dampers gave a firm ride. The engine of 4.4 litres had four overhead camshafts and the usual V12 layout. In 1976 the engine was enlarged to 4.8 litres and for the first time an automatic gearbox was offered by Ferrari as an option instead of five manual gears. The automatic gearbox had three speeds and was basically a GM box similar to that used by Rolls Royce. Much Connolly leather covers the seats and dashboard.

The roar of the six double-choke Webers and the 12 cylinder scream at high revs made this a very

sporting 2+2. The firm ride caused this big car to handle well and, like many other Ferrari cars, from the driver's perspective once inside at the wheel, they give the impression of being smaller than they really are. Over 241km/h (150mph) is a very creditable speed for nearly two tons of motor car, even if there are 340 horses on hand.

Fuel injection was fitted in 1979 and the

Below: Ferrari 365 GT4 2+2, chassis # 17127. Plenty of glass ensured excellent visibility, the rubber bumpers were innovative for 1972. Right: Ferrari 400 automatic had four rear lamps instead of the 365's six.

Below: This is an interior shot of the first 400 automatic to arrive in the UK. The T-handle for the General Motors' 3-speed automatic gearbox looks odd in a Ferrari.

53

model became known as the 400i. This was the first production Ferrari not to use Weber carburettors, and in this instance emissions, fuel consumption and power all improved. The biggest difference was the sound of the engine from inside; gone was the induction roar and everything suddenly seemed more civilized. The 5-speed version was still available though it could only be ordered in the ratio of 1·6. This figure says less about the 'sporting owners' but more about the world we live in. In the ten years since the 365 GT4 2+2 was first announced, only minor external changes had taken place. The rear light clusters were reduced from six to four, a small front spoiler was added, and 'bolt-on' wheels replaced the three eared 'knock offs'.

At the Geneva Show in 1985 the 412 was introduced. This was the final version of this car. The engine had been enlarged to 5 litres, ABS braking was standard, and while the general shape was unchanged, the boot line had been raised by 5cm (2in). When the 412 went out of production in 1989, the 'shape' had been with us for 17 years; it was time for a change.

Production figures	In production	Total produced
365	1972-76	525
400	1976-79	502
400i	1979-85	1308
412	1985-89	576

SPECIFICATION	365	400	400i	412
ENGINE	V12, 4390cc	V12, 4823cc	V12, 4823cc	V12, 4942cc
HORSEPOWER	320bhp @ 6200rpm	340bhp @ 6500rpm	310bhp @ 6400rpm	340bhp @ 6000rpm
TRANSMISSION	Manual 5-speed	Manual 5-speed/auto	Manual 5-speed/auto	Manual 5-speed/auto
CHASSIS	Steel tubular	Steel tubular	Steel tubular	Steel tubular
SUSPENSION	Independent all round *(all models)*			
BRAKES	Disc	Disc	Disc	Disc
TOP SPEED	241km/h (150mph)	240km/h (149mph)	240km/h (149mph)	249km/h (155mph)
ACCELERATION	0-96km/h (60mph): 7.1sec 0-161km/h (100mph):18sec	6.9sec 17.5sec	7.5sec N/A	6.4sec 16.1sec

Ferrari 412 automatic, chassis # 80652. The 412 was the final title for this shape. The 5-litre V12 engine gave 340bhp, the brakes had ABS and this model offered many other improvements over previous versions.

54

Ferrari 365 GT4BB, BB 512 & BB 512i

THE 'Boxer' was first seen on Pininfarina's stand at the Turin Motor Show in 1971 and it was not until the Geneva Show in 1973 that we first saw the BB on Ferrari's stand. This was not Ferrari's first mid-engined road car but it was the first mid-engined big berlinetta.

Ferrari's solution to mounting a large multi-cylinder engine amidships was to place the 4.4 litre flat 12 (or 180°V) on top of the gearbox and final drive. The drive shafts went out to each rear wheel from just before the end of the engine. The clutch was mounted on the flywheel, from where the drive went via drop gears to the gearbox. Four triple-choke Weber 40 1F3C carburettors stood in lines above the inlet ports of the two valve cylinder heads. Being a 'flat' engine its appearance could be likened to two straight-six cylinder engines on their sides sharing a common crankshaft. Four overhead cam shafts were driven from the front of the engine by two toothed belts. The belts needed checking every 19,300km (12,000 miles) and changing at approximately 40,000km (25,000 mile) intervals. This service item was easily executed after first removing the engine.

The coachwork was carried out in Modena by Scaglietti to Pininfarina's designs. The fixed centre section was steel and the large hinged engine cover, front bonnet and doors were skinned in aluminium. Above and behind the vertical rear window was a small aerofoil which disturbed the flow of air over the back of the car so that the carburettors could take in air. The overall shape of the design was so slippery that no air was available without this device. In practical terms it also acted as a 'handle' when opening and closing the engine cover. Six exhaust pipes surmounted by six round rear lights endowed the BB with an easily recognised rear aspect. Four headlights came up in front in two electrically operated nacelles.

A large pantograph arm carried the main wiper blade from one side of the screen to the other, whilst a tiny blade cleared the bit underneath that the bigger one missed. The sun visors were unusual in that small roller blinds were pulled down and fixed to the inside of the front screen with suction pads. The plain black-knobbed gear lever for selecting gears in its chrome gate and a leather-rimmed alloy steering wheel all looked familiar. The first 365 seats were trimmed in tweed which looked great (for a while). The round instruments were housed in square black frames and glowed red at night. A steel-tube frame supported double wishbone independent suspension all round with concentric coil springs and dampers, there being two suspension units on each side at the rear. The chassis layout made the 365 BB a more nimble and responsive car to drive than the Daytona; it was almost as quick but not so stable.

Left: Ferrari 365 GT4 BB, probably straight off the Motor Show stand in 1974. The Boxer had a rear-mounted flat 12.

SPECIFICATION	365 GT4BB	BB 512	BB 512i
ENGINE	180° V12, 4390cc	180° V12, 4942cc	180° V12, 4942cc
HORSEPOWER	344bhp @ 7000rpm	340bhp @ 6200rpm	340bhp @ 6000rpm
TRANSMISSION	Manual 5-speed	Manual 5-speed	Manual 5-speed
CHASSIS	Steel tubular	Steel tubular	Steel tubular
SUSPENSION	Independent all round (all models)		
BRAKES	Disc	Disc	Disc
TOP SPEED	274km/h (170mph)	274km/h (170mph)	274km/h (170mph)
ACCELERATION	0-96km/h (60mph): 5.3sec	6.2sec	5.4sec
	0-161km/h (100mph): 11.3sec	13.6sec	13.4sec

At the Paris Salon of 1976 the 365 BB became the BB 512 with a 5 litre engine, bigger rear wheels, a front spoiler, NACA duct for rear brake cooling and only four rear lights. Leather seats had been standard for some time by now. The larger engine made it an easier car to drive and modifications to the gear selection made operation of the gear lever feel like a good switch.

There was confusion and controversy in various magazines concerning the maximum speed and engine output of both 365 BB and the BB 512. The original press release was optimistic, and one of the later BB 512 road tests was plagued with water contaminating the petrol.

The final version of the Boxer was unveiled at the Paris Salon of 1981; there was not much visual difference but, as its new name implied, it had fuel injection. The BB 512i had 340bhp and a maximum speed of over 274km/h (170mph). In eleven years of Boxer production speeds and power had always been around the same level but the years brought refinement which made the 512i do it all with such ease and style.

Production figures	In production	Total produced
365 GT4BB	1973-76	387
BB 512	1976-81	929
BB 512i	1981-84	1007

Above: Ferrari BB 512i, chassis # 40331. The injection Boxer was an altogether more civilized car than its predecessors. Below: Interior of a BB 512 in 1979; the ribbed leather seats were very comfortable and the instruments glowed red at night.

Ferrari Dino 308 GT4 2+2

INTRODUCED at the Paris Salon in October 1973, this model was first seen in the UK some two weeks later at Earls Court. The first thing that I remember about the GT4 was how similar the driving position was to a 250 LM, the throttle pedal being almost under the steering column. The seats had a central strip of velour surrounded by plastic – this was very un-Ferrari in style. In front of the steering wheel, the instrument panel seemed to drop away to the nose, which was quite close to the base of the steeply raking screen.

Excellent forward and side vision was slightly spoilt by the rear flying buttresses. Two small rear seats showed that the Porsche 911 was in Ferrari's sights when the GT4 was drafted. The body designed by Bertone (the first and last non-Pininfarina design of a roadgoing Ferrari since the mid '50s) was made in Modena by Scaglietti. It was fabricated in steel with aluminium for the boot engine and front lid skins. The angular shape was not universally liked, probably because it was so unlike its stablemate, the curvaceous Dino 246.

The GT4 had a wonderful new engine though, which produced 255bhp at 7600rpm. This new engine was a 90 degree V8 with four overhead camshafts, hemispherical combustion chambers and a bore and stroke inherited straight from the Daytona. The installation was the same as for the Dino 246, in that the transverse mid-engine was mounted on top of its gearbox and differential and drove the rear wheels. The camshafts were driven by cog toothed belts just like the Boxer which débuted on the same day.

Below: An early example of a Ferrari Dino 308 GT4 2+2. The angular shape, designed by Bertone, was not to everybody's taste. Dino badges graced bonnet, wheels and horn button.

Left: A three-quarter rear view of the same red 308 2+2.
Below: Ferrari 308 GT4 2+2, chassis # 13366. A beautiful
shot of Bertone's small Ferrari, the only production Ferrari not
to be styled by Pininfarina since the mid '50s. In 1976 the
308 became a Ferrari and this picture shows that all the
badges subsequently had a prancing horse on them.

Double wishbone suspension all round, together with Michelin 205/70 VR14 radials, gave the GT4 excellent grip, and although the 'limit' was not often reached, its ultimate behaviour, particularly in the wet, could take one by surprise.

In the summer of 1976 the Dino 308 became a Ferrari which involved changing all badges from the 'landscape' Dino badge to the 'portrait' prancing horse. The driving position was improved and the front grille was extended over the fog lights to the same width as the front bumper. The familiar five-spoke alloy wheels were also introduced at this stage and were available with 16.5cm (6½in) rims as standard or 19cm (7½in) as an optional extra.

Most cars supplied in the UK had 19cm (7½in) rims from 1976 onwards. The steering when parking was noticeably heavier with these rims, but overall they improved an already great chassis.

The 308 GT4 was the first of the line of V8 Ferraris which have now become the backbone of production. History says that when the 308 replaced the 246 most people were disappointed aesthetically. But now that the Mondial has gone, the 308 GT4 will be the small 2+2 that true drivers will remember. The finish on the GT4 was mediocre although Ferrari, like all other car makers at the end of the 1970s, was making tremendous efforts towards improvements in resisting corrosion.

Production figures	In production	Total produced
Dino 308 GT 2+2	1973-80	2826

SPECIFICATION	DINO 308 GT 2+2
ENGINE	90° V8, 2926cc
HORSEPOWER	255bhp @ 7600rpm
TRANSMISSION	Manual 5 speed
CHASSIS	Steel tubular
SUSPENSION	Independent all round
BRAKES	Disc
TOP SPEED	248km/h (154mph)
ACCELERATION	0-96km/h (60mph): 6.9sec 0-161km/h (100mph): 18.1sec

Ferrari 308 GTB/GTS, Quattrovalvole & 328

OCTOBER 1975, Paris Salon, saw the debut of the most successful shape ever to wear the Cavallino Rampante emblem. Over 20,000 examples of all engine types and sizes were produced from 1975-1989. Pininfarina designed the two-seater berlinetta using the engine (now dry sump) and running gear from the 308 GT4 2+2. This new car was made on a traditional steel-tube chassis but its beautiful body was made in GRP (glass-reinforced-plastic). There had been fibreglass cars before but none of this quality – unfortunately most people equated fibreglass with 'kit cars' and after two years Scaglietti started making GTBs in steel. Moreover, they were heavier and had lost their dry sumps. The steel-bodied GTBs were soon joined by a spider version which was first shown to the world in 1977 at the first Motor Fair held at Earls Court, London.

The three litre, four-cam V8 (apart from the dry/wet sump) was more or less unchanged from the GT4 until March 1981 when legislation to protect the environment dictated the need to fit Bosch fuel injection in place of the four double-choke Webers.

The 308 GTB/Si was a shadow of its former self, having lost nearly forty horse power. Fortunately at Ferrari there was an executive named Eugenio Alzati who not only identified this dismal predicament for the world's best looking car, but did something about it. October 1982 saw the arrival of the 3-litre four-cam V8 with four valves per cylinder – 'quattrovalvole'. Honour and horsepower were restored.

The first 308 GTB was fitted with Michelin XWX 205/70 VR 14 tyres. The 308 GTBi had Michelin TRX which was a unique tyre with its own rim section and it therefore had to be replaced like for like. Pirelli P7 low profile tyres were available with special 40.6cm (16in) wheels as an optional extra for both GTB and GTBi. The 328 introduced in 1986 came with Goodyear NCTs 205/55 and 225/50 on 40.6cm (16in) wheels, 17.8cm (7in) wide at the front and 20.3cm (8in) at the back.

Below: The first RHD Ferrari 308 GTB, chassis # 19149.

SPECIFICATION	308 GTB/S	GTBi/Si	QV	328 GTB/S
ENGINE	90° V8, 2926cc	90° V8, 2926cc	90° V8, 2926cc	90° V8, 3185cc
HORSEPOWER	255bhp @ 7600rpm	214bhp @ 6600rpm	240bhp @ 7000rpm	270bhp @ 7000rpm
TRANSMISSION	Manual 5-speed	Manual 5-speed	Manual 5-speed	Manual 5-speed
CHASSIS	Steel tubular	Steel tubular	Steel tubular	Steel tubular
SUSPENSION	Independent all round *(all models)*			
BRAKES	Disc	Disc	Disc	Disc
TOP SPEED	246km/h (153mph)	237km/h (147mph)	254km/h (158mph)	254km/h (158mph)
ACCELERATION	0-96km/h (60mph): 6.4sec 0-161km/h (100mph): 15.9sec	7.9sec 22.1sec	5.7sec 14.3sec	5.5sec 13.8sec

Production figures	In production	Total produced
308 GTB/S	1975-80	2897(B)/3219(S)
GTBi/Si	1980-82	494(B)/1743(S)
QV	1982-85	748(B)/3042(S)
328 GTB/S	1985-89	1344(B)/6068(S)

The 328 was the ultimate evolution of this car with the engine size increased to 3185cc and maximum power of 270bhp at 7000rpm. The chassis was still much the same as it was in 1975 with double wishbones and concentric springs and shock absorbers all round. The brakes, which had always been superb, benefited from the addition of ABS (anti-lock) towards the end of production. Outwardly the 328 had a reworked front below the 'egg crate' grille, with a slightly deeper spoiler and a more rounded front, blending into the almost non-existent bumper. Generous-sized light units for side, direction and fog were placed either side of the grille. The car also had electrically controlled door mirrors, air conditioning, ABS, an all-leather interior, useful luggage space, a docile yet powerful engine, extremely high build quality and much else. In the late 1980s one expected all this. Some exotic cars even had electric seats with computerized memories, but the most marvellous thing about the Ferrari 328 GTB and GTS was that their character and charisma had not changed since the earlier days of 1975.

Below: Ferrari 308 GTS, chassis # 34995. The spider version of Pininfarina's beautiful 308 epitomized the small Ferrari of the '80s. The roof panel was easily removed or refitted by one person. Right: Engine of 308 GTB QV, chassis # 51249: less noise, more power and better response.

61

Ferrari Mondial 8, QV, 3.2 & Mondial t

THE ORIGINAL Ferrari Mondial was a four-cylinder 2 litre sports racer of which 39 were produced between 1954 and 1956. Pinin Farina and Scaglietti both made bodies for this early Ferrari sports car which had a Formula 2 engine.

The Mondial 8 was first seen in early 1980 at the Geneva Show. This was the replacement for the 308 GT4 2+2 and Pininfarina did a splendid job in making a long-wheelbase 2+2 look 'just like a Ferrari'. Everyone who bought a Mondial must have wished they had a berlinetta but practical reasons made them choose the bigger car. This was the first time that Ferrari had put fuel injection on the 3 litre V8, this being Bosch K-Jetronic injection, the same type that was already fitted to the twelve-cylinder Ferrari 400i. Also fitted to the Mondial was Marelli Digiplex electronic ignition giving greater flexibility,

no flat spots and reduced pollution. The result was 214bhp to propel nearly 1½ tons of car. The Mondial 8 did this in a very smooth way but was not exciting enough. No effort had been spared in the sumptuous finish which featured Connolly leather seats and dashboard, electric windows and air conditioning.

The Mondial had plenty of space inside and the rear seats were much more usable than those of most of its contemporaries. The ventilation and climate control and the adjustable steering column were refinements not before seen in a small Ferrari. The chassis was a typical Ferrari steel-tube design which had the unique capability of it being possible

to unbolt the back half and wheel out the engine/transmission and rear suspension. This 'service facility' also made it easier to build the Mondial in the first place. The all-round independent suspension was via double wishbones and concentric shock absorbers; unassisted rack and pinion steering gave the Mondial wonderful directional stability. The front suspension incorporated 'anti-dive' in its geometry. The instrumentation was more complete than usual, in that there were also warning lights for engine oil, gearbox oil, radiator fluid and windscreen washer levels together with warning lights for stop and tail light failures.

Left: Ferrari Mondial 8, chassis # 33737, offered more space, more weight and less speed. Right: 1984 Mondial cabriolet, chassis # 50513, showing 2+2 seating arrangement.

The Mondial was built using more advanced techniques than previous Ferrari cars. These included a new aluminium alloy for the engine and boot lid, new welding methods and much use of Zincrox, the pre-treated zincrometal sheet developed by Ferrari.

Late summer 1982 saw the new four-valves-per-cylinder engine – the 'quattrovalvole' – fitted to the Mondial. As with the 308s, this was a substantial improvement. In 1984 the Quattrovalvole was available as a cabriolet. The manually operated roof incorporating the coupé's flying buttresses was designed by Pininfarina and again made in Modena by Scaglietti.

The Frankfurt Motor Show 1985 was a busy time for Ferrari. All the V8-engined cars had their bores and strokes increased to give 3185cc and a boost in power to 270bhp at 7000rpm. The new 3.2 Mondial was yet again a useful improvement on the 3 litre version.

Geneva 1989 saw Ferrari announce the Mondial t – this was the first appearance of the V8 four-valve engine bored and stroked to 3405cc. The four-valve V8 was almost the only familiar part of the specification. The engine had been turned 90° in the chassis and now had its crankshaft on the car's longitudinal axis. The engine was so low now, it was almost out of sight in the tall Mondial engine bay. The boot at the back was the same size, so where was the gearbox? The 5-speed gearbox stayed where it had always been. This arrangement called 'trasversale' meaning 'transverse' had been tried by Ferrari in Formula 1 cars of the mid-1970s and this was what the letter 't' in the name signified. It all resulted in a lower centre of gravity and better power to weight ratio though unfortunately a cable-operated gearshift ruined one of Ferrari's most characteristic features. The suspension got electronically adjustable Bilsten gas units which changed pressure with speed and cornering forces. Power steering was a hardly noticeable addition.

SPECIFICATION	Mondial 8	Quattrovalvole*	Mondial 3.2*	Mondial t*
ENGINE	90° V8, 2926cc	90° V8, 2926cc	90° V8, 3185cc	90° V8, 3405cc
HORSEPOWER	214bhp @ 6600rpm	240bhp @ 7000rpm	270bhp @ 7000rpm	300bhp @ 7200rpm
TRANSMISSION	Manual 5-speed	Manual 5-speed	Manual 5-speed	Manual 5-speed
CHASSIS	Steel tubular	Steel tubular	Steel tubular	Steel tubular
SUSPENSION	Independent all round *(all models)*			
BRAKES	Disc	Disc	Disc	Disc
TOP SPEED	225km/h (140mph)	235km/h (146mph)	238km/h (148mph)	249km/h (155mph)
ACCELERATION	0-96km/h (60mph): 7sec	6.4sec	6.3sec	5.6sec
	0-161km/h (0-100mph): 21sec	16.2sec	15.8sec	13.9sec
* including cabriolet				

Production figures	In production	Total produced
Mondial 8	1980-82	703
Quattrovalvole	1982-85	1774
Mondial 3.2	1985-89	1797
Mondial t	1989-92	N/A

Ferrari 288 GTO & Evoluzione

THE 288 GTO was built for a number of reasons – to make money, to try out new ideas, to race and to promote the name of Ferrari by making a 'Supercar'.

The title 288 GTO indicated a 2.8 litre, 8 cylinder engine and the 'O' stood for 'omologato' which means approved. (The intended approval was for the 2.8 litre turbo engine to run in the up to 4 litre class of Group B racing – 2.8 multiplied by the turbo coefficient of 1.4 makes 3920cc). It also nostalgically recalled the fabulously successful 250 GTO of the early 1960s. In some ways giving the new untried car such an awesome name was tempting fate. As it happened, the Group B regulations were changed and the new 'GTO' never saw a circuit. This, however, should in no way detract from the reputation of the new 'Supercar' which was first seen publicly at the Geneva International Motor Show of 1984. At the Motor Show in October of the same year, the 288 GTO shared its debut in England with the Testarossa. As all the 288s were sold, it was almost hidden, whilst the Testarossa was on a raised dais.

The 288 derives from the 308 GTB. Some would say the bonnet badge was all they had in common, but that is to deny the wonderful qualities of Pininfarina's GTB and Ferrari's straightforward and robust engineering. Doctor Harvey Postelthwaite, the English Ferrari Grand Prix engineer, introduced composites to Ferrari and the 288 was their first road car to experiment with such

things, albeit in a small way. A typical composite structure is formed by a reinforcing material such as high tensile Kevlar fibres which, when immersed in a plastic matrix, give rise to a new material which is stronger and lighter than aluminium. The complete chassis and bodywork of a modern racing car is made by this technique using an autoclave moulding process with carbon, Kevlar, glass, nomex, light alloys, epoxy resins and adhesives. Some parts of the 288 employ these methods and materials to reduce weight and increase strength.

The 288 engine is a 90° V8 with four overhead camshafts operating 32 valves; twin IHI turbochargers feed through two Behr heat exchangers and Weber-Marelli provide an electronic injection and ignition system. Water-cooled, using a dry sump, the light alloy block and cylinder heads

are all placed longitudinally in a steel-tube chassis. A twin plate clutch drives the 5-speed all-synchromesh transaxle which is placed behind the engine in the classic racing car layout.

The suspension is by wishbones and coil springs with coaxial shock absorbers – the wishbones themselves being beautifully fabricated from tubular steel both front and rear. The body, which has its origins in the 308 GTB, is made of glass-reinforced-plastic composite materials. The actual car is almost 20cm (8in) wider than the 308 thanks to Goodyear NCT tyres on 25.4 x 40.6cm (10x16in) wheels at the rear and 20.3 x 40.6cm (8x16in) wheels at the front with bulging wheel arches to accommodate them.

SPECIFICATION	228 GTO
ENGINE	V8, twin turbo, 2855cc
HORSEPOWER	400bhp @ 7000rpm
TRANSMISSION	Manual 5-speed
CHASSIS	Steel tubular
SUSPENSION	Independent all round
BRAKES	Disc
TOP SPEED	304km/h (189mph)
ACCELERATION	0-96km/h (60mph): 4.9sec 0-200km/h (124mph): 15.2sec

A roll bar is incorporated in the cockpit which houses a pair of beautifully trimmed adjustable seats, the centres of which could have come straight from a Daytona. The black leather-covered steering wheel, gear lever, minor controls and instruments except for the boost gauge and the 320km/h (200mph) speedometer all come from the 308 GTB.

The acceleration was staggering by any standards and one had to be careful with the throttle even in the dry.

The 288 did not go racing because the rules were changed, but not before Ferrari had started to develop a racing version – called 'Evoluzione'. This version had a 40 per cent lighter chassis, 650bhp and would do 370km/h (230mph). This prototype was built by Michelotto of Padua and was to form the basis of the car we now know as the F40.

Production figures	In production	Total produced
288 GTO	1984-86	273

Left Ferrari 288 GTO. With 400bhp and its lightweight body, it is such a pity the 288 never went racing. Top: One of a handful of 288 GTO Evoluziones which were used as mobile test beds to develop the F40. Above: Engine bay of a 288 GTO showing the twin turbo-charged V8 engine.

Ferrari Testarossa, 512 TR & F512M

THE LAUNCH of the Testarossa in October 1984 in Paris was done in a very grand way, well befitting such a Grand Touring car. The name 'Testarossa' came from the Ferrari sports racing cars of the late 1950s. Most Ferrari engine cam covers are finished in a crackle back paint or, in the case of early Lampredi engines, plain aluminium. However, the 500 Mondial, a four-cylinder, two litre sports racer became known as the 500 Testa Rossa as its horsepower was increased and its cam covers were painted red – presumably to distinguish it from the less powerful 500 Mondial – (in Italian testa = head, rossa = red). The fashion of painting cam covers red continued with the 250 Testa Rossa V12-engined sports cars and the last Ferrari sports racer to use this nomenclature was the TRI 330 LM,

which in 1962 was the last front-engined car to win at Le Mans.

In Paris, over twenty years later, everyone knew what a Testa Rossa had been, such was its fame. The new car used a single word to distinguish itself as Testarossa. There were underlying similarities with the BB 512i, but the most important differences were new four-valves-per-cylinder heads (with red cam covers of course!) and a new body designed and made by Pininfarina. The familiar flat 12 or 'Boxer' engine was retained, but it and the independent rear suspension was attached to a separate part of the chassis which 'unbolted' from in front of the engine for ease of maintenance. The large cooling radiator that the Boxer had in its nose had been removed, and two

new radiators were to be found one each side in front of the rear wheels. The air intakes for these new radiators were incorporated in the doors and covered with horizontal slats. At the edge of the door the slats were held together with a vertical member whose profile was aerofoil-shaped and which increased the speed of the air going into the radiators. The traditional front grille retained its looks but not its function and now only provided air for cooling the front brakes and the air conditioner's heat exchanger. The horizontally opposed twelve-cylinder engine had a block and heads made in light alloy with the pistons and aluminium cylinder liners coated in Nicasil. Bosch K-Jetronic fuel injection looked after the induction.

The bodywork of the Testarossa was made of aluminium with the exception of the centre section and doors which were made of Zincrox, Ferrari's patent rustproof steel. The large single external rearview mirror was not an elegant feature. Luggage space provided under the front lid and behind the seats housed special handmade suitcases from Modena firm Schedoni.

After the most successful sales of any twelve-cylinder Ferrari during a span of eight years, improvements were made which saw the Ferrari 512 TR launched in Los Angeles in January 1992. The

Left: Ferrari Testarossa. Pininfarina's new wide shape for the berlinetta; side strakes cover air intakes for the side-mounted engine cooling radiators.

F 512 M

Left: Ferrari F 512 M. Gone are the pop-up headlights, but that enormous number plate must upset the air flow
Above: A 1990 Testarossa in 'Bianco' white which makes this car 'grow' and that makes it appear too big!

 67

changes included new seats, some interior rearrangement, engine modifications that increased power by some 38bhp and suspension tuning that brought the chassis in line with performance. New wheels were fitted with giant 235/40 ZR 18 front and 295/35 ZR 18 rear, and the 'get you home' bicycle type spare wheel was abandoned in favour of no spare at all. This increased luggage space.

At the Paris Salon of 1994 Ferrari changed the name again to F 512 M. This variant featured a gain in horsepower, a reduction in weight, new headlights, switchable anti lock brakes and new Speedline wheels.

SPECIFICATION	TESTAROSSA	512 TR	F 512 M
ENGINE	Flat 12, 4942cc	Flat 12, 4942cc	Flat 12, 4942cc
HORSEPOWER	390bhp @ 6300rpm	428bhp @ 6750rpm	440bhp @ 6750rpm
TRANSMISSION	Manual 5-speed	Manual 5-speed	Manual 5-speed
CHASSIS	Steel tubular	Steel tubular	Steel tubular
SUSPENSION	Independent all round *(all models)*		
BRAKES	Disc	Disc	Disc
TOP SPEED	291km/h (181mph)	312km/h (194mph)	315km/h (196mph)
ACCELERATION	0-96km/h (60mph): 5.8sec	5.1sec	4.8sec
	0-161km/h (100mph): 12./sec	10.6sec	10.2sec

Production figures	In production	Total produced
Testarossa	1984-92	7177
512 TR	1992-94	N/A
F 512 M	1994-	N/A

Ferrari 512 TR, chassis # 94516. Much more than a face-lifted Testarossa – more power, bigger brakes and wheels, a new nose, new seats, and no spare wheel. This had been dispensed with in favour of a pressurized glue cylinder to seal and inflate a punctured tyre.

Ferrari F40

THE F40 was the last car 'ordered' by Enzo Ferrari and was so called to celebrate 40 years of building cars. It was conceived in the summer of 1986 when Ing. Ferrari is reputed to have said 'Let's make something special for next year's celebrations in the way we used to do it' meaning putting a more powerful engine into a lighter version of an existing chassis.

The results were ready within a year and had been helped enormously by the development of the 288 GTO Evoluziones which did many hours and miles testing turbocharged V8 engines. Also running at the same time was a long-wheelbase 2+2 cabriolet with a front engine built by Scaglietti using composite materials in the chassis. The nose came from a Mondial and the mechanicals from a 412. This prototype proved that the strength and lightness of composites would stand up to the rigours of road use. The four-wheel-drive prototype with the four litre V8 (408), which was developed by Mauro Forghieri, also had a hand in the development of the F40. The four-wheel-drive, which used a fluid flywheel to control wheel spin, has not yet been used on a production Ferrari.

Many other aspects of this development vehicle were unusual, such as the composite body panels whose ingredients included polyamide fibre, polyurethane and fibre-reinforced plastics. Using ideas from these prototypes, the F40 was a mixture of traditional and advanced ideas. The chassis was very traditional, but the scuttle and door sills had been integrated in stiffening panels made from composites. The huge cost of making a composite monocoque had been deferred. The suspension, independent front and rear, was by double wishbones and coaxial shock absorbers. The shock absorbers could also control the ground clearance via a switch on the dashboard. Unassisted rack and pinion steering conveyed great confidence to the driver. The brakes, ventilated radially and drilled

SPECIFICATION	F40
ENGINE	V8, twin turbo, 2936cc
HORSEPOWER	478bhp @ 7000rpm
TRANSMISSION	Manual 5-speed
CHASSIS	Steel tubular
SUSPENSION	Independent all round
BRAKES	Disc
TOP SPEED	325km/h (202mph)
ACCELERATION	0-96km/h (60mph): 4.1sec 0-161km/h (100mph): 7.8sec

were attached to the hubs via aluminium bells which allowed for expansion and contraction during temperature changes. No servo was fitted to the dual system which employed four pot calipers at each corner.

The F40 was the first road car to be equipped with bag tanks; these are fuel tanks made from rubber and are more commonly found in aeroplanes and racing cars. The 5-speed gearbox and limited slip differential was very similar to that fitted to the 288 GTO, and also had a pair of drop gears to lower the centre of gravity. The alloy centre-lock wheels were usually fitted with Pirelli P zero tyres 245/40 ZR 17 front and 335/35 ZR 17 at the rear. There was no spare wheel or even the means for removing a tyre in the event of a puncture. Drivers had to put their faith in a pressurized bottle of repair liquid made by AGIP. The engine was a full three litre development of the

Opposite: Ferrari F40, chassis # 77289. Top: Spartan interior showing drilled pedals and Kevlar seat. Right: Rear view showing full-width rear wing.

288 GTO and proved to be extremely reliable. Pininfarina's no-compromise performance bodywork was first shown to the Concessionaires at Maranello in July 1987 and then publicly at the Frankfurt Show. The 288 Evoluzione was often featured in the motoring press before July 1987 keeping the Ferrari faithful happy with results of track tests and other stories. Before it came out the F40 was indeed a well kept secret.

The F40 was a truly magnificent car to look at, to drive and to dream about. It appeared on the market at the most extraordinary time when speculation in the automobile world was going mad; the first F40s to be delivered demanded premiums of up to three times their cost. Like all cars, a second-hand Ferrari used to be worth less than a new one, but in the late 1960s the acknowledged masterpieces began to hold their value better than cash. In the 1980s the idea that cars could be 'investments' had really caught on among both

enthusiasts and speculators, and prices rose to giddy heights. The bubble burst eventually in early 1990 and prices continue to drift except in the case of the very finest examples.

Production figures	In production	Total produced
F40	1988-91	1315

Ferrari 348 tb/ts, GTB/S & Spider

THE 348 was first seen and tried by Ferrari's Concessionaires at Maranello on 1st September 1989, prior to its first public appearance at the Frankfurt Show of the same year. Pininfarina had created a new 'small' car to replace the much loved 308 which was now a fourteen-year-old design.

The 348 was the first Ferrari to be designed without a comprehensive tubular chassis, the frame consisting of stamped steel sheet welded by robots. The resulting chassis was torsionally superior and dimensionally more accurate. The longitudinally mounted dry sump engine and transmission were attached to a tubular sub-frame fixed at the back of the main platform. The gearbox with five synchronized forward gears was mounted transversally between the engine and the rear-mounted clutch and below the limited slip differential. A quill shaft transmitted the drive from crankshaft via the clutch to gearbox. The gearchange on a Ferrari was usually an inimitable feature – a little slow perhaps when cold, but it was extraordinarily precise. However, the cable-operated gear change of the 348 failed to impress. The V8 engine which had four overhead camshafts and four valves per cylinder developed 300bhp at 7200rpm from 3405cc.

The block and heads were made of aluminium and the steel cylinder liners were coated with Nicasil. The engine cooling radiators were mounted amidships with air intakes on each flank. The Bosch Motronic M 2.5 system controlled both ignition and injection. The suspension was independent front and rear with the usual wishbones, coil springs and coaxial gas-filled shock absorbers. The collapsible and adjustable steering column controlled rack and pinion steering. The front suspension incorporated 'anti-dive' and the 43.2cm (17in) wheels housed large ventilated discs which together with aluminium calipers, ABS and servo assistance provided excellent stopping power. The bodywork was made from steel and aluminium and bore a definite family likeness to the Testarossa, particularly with regard to the side air intakes and the general frontal treatment. Such items as ventilation and air conditioning were greatly improved even if over-complicated with digital temperature read-out and sixteen control buttons! The title 348 tb signified a 3.4 litre 8 cylinder engine while 't' stood for 'trasversale' which described how the gearbox was positioned across the chassis. This arrangement had been tried successfully by Ferrari in the 312T Formula One cars of the mid-1970s, although the 312T had inboard brakes and the clutch between engine and transmission. The 'b' stood for berlinetta.

Left: Ferrari 348 Spider, chassis # 99058. The clean lines of the fully open Spider were made possible by the use of the new, stiffer chassis of the 348.

Below: Ferrari 3.4-litre V8 engine with transverse 5-speed gearbox, limited slip differential and clutch. Bottom: Ferrari 348 tb, chassis # 82982.

SPECIFICATION	348 TB & TS	GTB/S & SPIDER
ENGINE	V8, 3405cc	V8, 3405cc
HORSEPOWER	300bhp @ 7200rpm	320bhp @ 7200rpm
TRANSMISSION	Manual 5-speed	Manual 5-speed
CHASSIS	Steel platform & tubes	Steel platform & tubes
SUSPENSION	Independent all round	Independent all round
BRAKES	Disc	Disc
TOP SPEED	275km/h (171mph)	275km/h (171mph)
ACCELERATION	0-96km/h (60mph): 5.6sec	5.3sec
	0-161km/h (100mph): 13.3sec	13sec

to the increased rigidity of the 348 chassis, was a good fit. The 95 litre (21 gallon) fuel tank was a single unit placed behind the seats in front of the engine. This was the optimum place, within the wheelbase, to reduce the effect on handling as the fuel load changes.

There was a name change in 1993 – the two cars were now called 348 GTB and 348 GTS with little change other than an extra 20bhp. The 348 Spider, unveiled to the world at a unique event in Hollywood in February 1993, was available for those who wanted real open air driving.

At the same time as the berlinetta was announced, an 's' spider appeared too. The spider had a removable panel in the roof which stowed behind the seats when not in use and which, thanks

Production figures	In production	Total produced
348 TB & TS	1989-93	N/A
GTB/S & Spider	1993-94	N/A

Ferrari F355 Berlinetta, Spider & GTS

AS FERRARI model names go, the F355 adds another twist – it signifies a 3.5 litre engine with 5 valves per cylinder. The adding of 91cc to the 348 engine does not sound much in itself, but it turned into a 60bhp increase. This, if you like, is all that the average economy car can muster from 1000cc.

The block of the 355 engine had Nicasil coated steel liners and forged alloy pistons which were connected to the crankshaft via titanium alloy conrods usually seen only on Formula One cars. The cylinder heads were pure race-bred with three inlet and two exhaust valves per cylinder, and were quite unlike the 348. Four overhead camshafts operated hydraulic tappets and the valve springs were designed to operate at 10,000 rpm. The Bosch M 2.7 engine management system, a new exhaust system which reduced back pressure at high revs and had three catalytic converters, and a compression ratio of 11.1:1, all combined to endow the F355 engine with over 108bhp per litre – an incredible output for a road car.

The chassis retained the pressed steel platform of the 348 with a tubular rear structure which supported engine, transmission and rear suspension. The transmission looks the same as a 348, but now has six closely spaced ratios and a stronger clutch inside a magnesium alloy housing. The suspension, which was independent all round with double wishbones, had Bilstein shock absorbers, which were continuously adjustable via

electronic sensors according to the speed and attitude of the car. The result was an enormous improvement over the 348 and it took the F355 into an altogether higher league of handling.

Very often the best technical improvements are unseen and the F355's undertray is such an example. Instead of air pressure building up under the car to the detriment of handling, the F355 was a 'ground effects' car with air channelled into ducts causing negative lift and so increasing its adhesion to the road. The F355's rack and pinion steering had the unusual addition of power assistance, and the ABS braking system was fitted with an on/off switch. The bodywork had subtle smoothing changes. Also the side strakes were removed from

the radiator intakes and traditional uncluttered circular rear lamps were fitted. Together with the berlinetta, a GTS to the same specification has also been available and in May 1995, the Spider version was unveiled in Monte Carlo. The folding hood designed by Pininfarina was electrically operated, as were the two Connolly leather seats.

Production figures	In production	Total produced
F355	1994-	N/A

Below: Ferrari F355 GTS. The new 3.5-litre V8 with five valves per cylinder is shown here in GTS form impressing its occupants, at the Goodwood Motor Racing circuit, with its superb handling and effortless power.

Right: Ferrari F355 berlinetta, chassis # 102296.
The most impressive 'small' car in the world.

Right: Ferrari F355 Spider. The pressed steel platform
chassis of the F355 proves a stiffer proposition than the
tubes of the earlier cars.

SPECIFICATION	F355
ENGINE	V8, 3496cc
HORSEPOWER	380bhp @ 8250rpm
TRANSMISSION	Manual 6-speed
CHASSIS	Steel platform & tubes
SUSPENSION	Independent all round
BRAKES	Disc
TOP SPEED	298km/h (185mph)
ACCELERATION	0-96km/h (60mph): 4.6sec
0-161km/h (100mph): 10.6sec

Ferrari 456 GT 2+2

IN LATE summer 1992 Garage Francorchamps celebrated forty years of being the Ferrari Concessionaire for Belgium. Proprietor/ founder Jacques Swaters was honoured by Ferrari in having the new 456 GT 2+2 unveiled at his FF40 event. The title 456 recalled Ferrari's more traditional nomenclature whereby cc per cylinder times twelve equals the engine capacity. Pininfarina was responsible for the beautiful coachwork which was his first completely new front-engined Ferrari for 20 years.

Pininfarina had not forgotten how to draw front-engined Ferraris and the 456 had both historic and modern elements in it, reminding one of earlier cars in the rear three-quarter view, and a thoroughly modern nose. Hot air escaped from the engine compartment through huge reverse scoops behind the front wheels. The new five-spoke wheels first seen on the 512 TR were now used on the 456, carrying 255/45 ZR 17 front tyres and 285/40 ZR 17 rear tyres. A rear-mounted aerodynamic aid was incorporated below the rear bumper; it only operated above a certain speed to increase downforce. The bodywork is made of aluminium with a small amount of composite in the headlamp nacelles and front bonnet. The aluminium body is chemically bonded to the steel chassis via a special material called FERAN. The chassis is made from steel tubes in the traditional Ferrari way, with independent suspension by double wishbones at each corner. Electronically controlled shock absorbers and coil springs continually ensure that maximum comfort and security are maintained.

Below: Ferrari 456 GT, chassis # 98402. It was the first all-new, front-engined Ferrari in 20 years. Glamour shot of the engine shows 65° V12 of 5.5-litres.

There is also a hydraulically controlled self-levelling device in the rear suspension and ZF speed-sensitive, power-assisted rack and pinion steering.

The completely new V12 engine of 5.5 litres capacity had a 65 degree included angle between the two lines of six cylinders, a little wider than on previous V12s. Four overhead camshafts operate

SPECIFICATION	456 GT 2+2
ENGINE	65° V12, 5474cc
HORSEPOWER	442bhp @ 6250rpm
TRANSMISSION	Manual 6-speed, auto 4 speed
CHASSIS	Steel tubular
SUSPENSION	Independent all round
BRAKES	Disc
TOP SPEED	299km/h (186mph)
ACCELERATION	0-96km/h (60mph): 5.2sec 0-161km/h (100mph): 11.6sec

four valves per cylinder and all the engine castings are in aluminium. A dry sump oil system with two scavenge pumps helped to lower the bonnet line. This was the largest capacity Ferrari engine ever, with the exception of the 612 and 712 Can-Am racers of 1970. Nearly 306km/h (190mph) was the claimed maximum speed for the new 456 GT which uses a 6-speed, rear-mounted transaxle.

A 4-speed electronically controlled automatic transmission is now available and this must be good news for sales as less than 25 per cent of this car's predecessor had manual boxes. The automatic 3-speed torque convertor which was used in the 400, 400i and 412 was a General Motors box also used by Rolls-Royce for their powerful , but fairly slow-revving V8. The new box has had to be designed specifically for the 456 not only because of the high-revving nature of this latest V12 with 442bhp at 6250rpm, but also because of the fact that the

gearbox is in unit with the differential in an unusual configuration. The new transmission was designed in collaboration with FFD Ricardo, a British company, and manufactured in America by a subsidiary.

Production figures	In production	Total produced
456 GT 2+2	1992-	N/A

Ferrari F50

THIS IS the third supercar to come from Ferrari in ten years. Naturally it is technically more advanced, faster and more expensive than the previous models. The F50 is without doubt closer to racing car technology, whereas the 288 and the F40 were more closely related to road cars. With hindsight, Ferrari could have sold a few more 288s without diluting its prestige and maybe a few less

F40s (there are more F40s around than Daytonas, for example). The stated aim to make only 349 Ferrari F50s will ensure that enough are sold to make money without creating an oversupply situation.

The success of both the 288 and F40, together with customer demand, led Ferrari into the F50 – but F50 is more special. For a start it has a V12 engine (will F60 be a V10?) which goes to the

Ferrari F50. This 1996 photograph shows an early F50 at Silverstone. Pininfarina's line is in evidence again, much developed in the wind tunnel.

core of tradition, and this is not just a development of a road engine but one that has its origins in Formula One. The engine, whose block is in cast iron, acts as a stressed member and bolts to the back of the carbonfibre chassis.

The clutch and transmission housing, which bolts directly onto the back of the engine, provides pick-up points for the rear suspension and bodywork. The suspension, by double wishbones front and rear, uses a push-rod system developed in Formula One to operate the inboard-mounted coaxial springs and dampers. The dampers, developed with Bilstein, are electronically controlled and managed by an ECU (Electronic Control Unit) which reacts to acceleration, steering and other attitudes of the car. To complement the electronics, there is no compliance in the suspension pivot points ensuring maximum precision in operation. Ferrari have gone to great lengths to achieve the minimum unsprung weight, not only by using push rod suspension, but by making components such as the rear uprights in a special hot-forged aluminium alloy, using aluminium disc bells front and rear, plus aluminium four pot brake calipers and hubs in titanium.

The five-spoke road wheels are a one-piece design and are cast in magnesium with a single hexagonal fixing, 45.7 x 21.6cm (18 x 8^1/$_2$in) front and 45.7 x 33cm (18 x 13in) at the rear. Goodyear made a special tyre for the F50 called 'Fiorano'. The chassis is made entirely of Cytec Aerospace carbonfibre and weighs only 102kg (225lb). Light alloy attachment points are bonded into it for front suspension, engine and bodywork. The rubber bag tank of 105 litres (23 gallons) capacity is situated

SPECIFICATION	F50
ENGINE	V12, 4700cc
HORSEPOWER	520bhp @ 8500rpm
TRANSMISSION	Manual 6-speed
CHASSIS	Composite tub
SUSPENSION	Independent all round
BRAKES	Disc
TOP SPEED	325km/h (202mph)
ACCELERATION	0-96km/h (60mph): 3.7sec Standing km: 21.7sec Standing mile: 30.3sec

hi-tech with leather-covered composite seats and beautiful carbon fibre mouldings. The dashboard incorporates instruments managed by a micro-computer including an LCD which shows which gear you are in!

Production figures	In production	Total produced
F50	1995-	N/A

Below: Ferrari F50, chassis # 103462. This shows the 'barchetta' mode with top removed and headrests in place. Right: Engine bay and rear suspension.

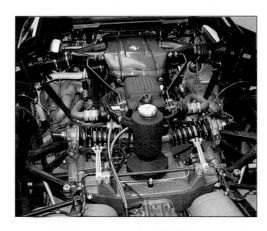

low down between the back of the seats and the engine within the carbonfibre chassis.

The engine is a direct development of the 3.5 litre naturally aspirated Formula One unit of 1990, and has been enlarged to 4.7 litres. Four overhead camshafts operate five valves per cylinder. It is dry sump, with a compression ratio of 11.3:1 and uses a Bosch Motronic 2.7 electronic engine management system. The forged alloy pistons and titanium con rods, magnesium gear box casing and bodywork made entirely from composite material clearly show the F50's heritage.

The bodywork, designed by Pininfarina, is entirely functional, yet echoes elements of past glorious Ferrari sports racers. Negative lift is achieved by means of the 'ground effects' undertray and the rear wing. The radiator hot air exits also help to keep weight on the front. The most unusual aspect of the F50 bodywork is its dual role – it has a hard top which makes the berlinetta, and when removed it becomes a barchetta with two rounded head rests and roll bars. The interior is sumptuous

Glossary/Index